Copyright © 2024 by Dylan and Friends Publishing Company. All rights reserved.

Library of Congress Control Number: 2024900351

No part of this book may be reproduced, scanned, or distributed in any printed or electronic form without permission. Please do not participate in or encourage piracy of copyrighted materials in violation of the author's rights. Thank you for respecting the hard work of this author.

This is a work of fiction. Names, characters, places, and incidents either are the product of the author's imagination or are used fictitiously, and any resemblance to locales, events, business establishments, or actual persons—living or dead—is entirely coincidental.

STAY INFORMED

I'd love to stay in touch! You can email me at kathleen@kathleentroy.com

For updates about new releases, as well as exclusive promotions, visit my website and sign up for the VIP mailing list. Head there now to receive a free story

www.kathleentroy.com

Enjoying the series? Help others discover *Dylan's Dog Squad* by sharing with a friend.

ALSO BY KATHLEEN TROY

Dylan's Dog Squad Series

Dylan's Dilemma

Dylan's Dream

Dylan's Villain

Dylan's Hawaiian Ghost ('O ka 'uhane Hawai'i 'o Dylan)

Dylan's Nose Knows

Coming soon: Dylan's Millions

Never Believe Series

Never Believe in Luck Twice
(Prologue/short story to Never Believe a Lie Twice)

Never Believe a Lie Twice

Coming soon: Never Believe a Con Artist Twice

DYLAN'S NOSE KNOWS

DYLAN'S DOG SQUAD
BOOK 5

KATHLEEN TROY

DYLAN AND FRIENDS PUBLISHING COMPANY

To Dylan,
Happy birthday, Little Buddy!
XOXO

Only you can make yourself happy.
-Dylan

Dreams are like sports. Unless you get out and play,
you got nothing to talk about later.
-Dylan

ONE

"Okay, Little Buddy." Casey leaned closer to Dylan and pointed to the kids on the outdoor basketball court. "The score is tied, sixty-eight to sixty-eight."

Sixty-eight is a lot. I can only count to ten.

"Go Brea Wildcats!" Sumo was on his feet, hands cupped to his mouth. "You can do it!"

"This is it." Casey stretched out his long legs and pulled Dylan onto his lap. "We have to get the ball and make a basket if we're going to win."

Dylan sat up for a better look and saw Jake move in. *Get the ball!* Dylan wiggled his buns and pranced his front paws on Casey's legs.

"Move it, Jake!" Sumo shouted.

Hurry! Dylan's heart hitched when Jake took the ball away from the kid in the red and black jersey. *Yay!*

Jake shot down the court.

Dylan watched Jake bouncing the ball and switching hands as he went. Dylan looked at his furry paws and sighed. *I wish I could bounce a ball like that.*

Players in red and black jerseys crowded in and waved

their hands in front of Jake. Jake dodged them, kept control of the ball, and kept going.

Jake made it to the hoop, gripped the ball with both hands and jumped. The crowd went wild stomping their feet, shouting, and whistling.

"Brea Wildcats won!" Casey showed Dylan his hand. "High five!"

High four! Dylan slapped his paw on Casey's hand and wagged his stubby tail. *Basketball is fun.*

Sumo was on his feet pumping his fist into the air and shouting, "Great play, Jake!"

Arf!

On the court eight sweaty kids in red and black jerseys gave a limp high five to eight sweaty kids in blue and gold jerseys. All looked ready to collapse. One boy yanked his jersey over his head and used it to wipe his face. Another kid put his hands on his hips and walked in slow small circles. Others bent over at the waist, hands on knees.

Coach Reynolds blew his whistle. "Hustle, guys! Get your gear." He left the sidelines and walked over to Casey, Dylan, and Sumo. "What do you think?"

"Great game." Casey hugged Dylan. "Thanks for making Dylan your mascot."

Dylan looked down at himself and snuffled his blue and gold jersey. *This is so cool. I've never had a jersey before.*

"Dylan's Dog Squad is famous." Coach Reynolds gave Dylan's muzzle a friendly scratch. "With this little guy as the Brea Wildcats' mascot, our summer games will draw a crowd." He gestured to the people packing up and leaving. "This is our biggest turnout yet. We owe you."

Jake jogged over, still carrying the basketball. "Hey, Coach."

"Good game." Coach Reynolds checked his watch. "I'm out of here." He nodded to them. "Catch you later."

"See ya." Jake waved goodbye and then tossed the basketball into the air. When the ball landed neatly on the tip of his right index finger, Jake gave it a soft left-handed slap.

Wow! Dylan watched the basketball spin. *I wish I could do that.* He looked down at his front paws. *I wish I had fingers.*

Jake grinned at Dylan and let the ball drop on the ground. "Want to play?"

Yes! Dylan wiggled off Casey's lap and jumped off the bleachers. He pounced on the ball, landing chest first and tried wrapping his front legs around it. The ball rolled. *Agh!* Dylan rolled with it, hugging the ball to him before falling over onto his side. *This is a big ball.* The ball slipped away from him, bounced up and hit him in the snout. *Ow!* Dylan rubbed his nose with his front paws and shook himself out. *Forget it. A baseball is better. It fits in my mouth.*

Casey patted the metal bleachers next to him. Dylan hopped up, flopped down and spread out. He nuzzled Casey's backpack and panted. *Playing basketball is thirsty business.*

"Hold on." Casey brought out Dylan's collapsible water dish and poured water into it.

"Got it all on video." Sumo showed his cell phone to Jake and laughed. "Like when you missed the shot in the second quarter, tripped over your big feet and landed on your butt."

Jake lunged for the phone. "Gimme that."

"Too late." Sumo held it up and away. "Social media is all over this. You've already gotten like fifty hits."

"Thanks a lot."

Sumo shoved the cell phone into his shorts pocket and grinned. "At least you won the game."

"Guys," Casey gave them the time out sign, "let's celebrate and go to Big Belly's for pizza."

Dylan's head whipped up from his water dish and water flew off his muzzle. *Big Belly's cheese pizza is my favorite.* His stomach growled. *I like their tomato and mozzarella pizza too. And their mushroom pizza.* He sighed happily. *I like them all.*

"Sounds great but I got to go home first." Jake pulled his sticky shirt away from himself. "Man, it's hot."

No kidding. Dylan went back to his dish and finished it off.

Sumo rubbed a hand over his stomach. "I'm starving now."

Jake laughed. "You're always starving."

Casey's cell phone vibrated, and he read the screen. "This is weird. Mom says some guy just dropped in and I have to go home. She wants Sumo to come too." He texted something back and slipped his cell phone into his pocket. "We'll meet you at Big Belly's."

"Sure." Jake waved and took off.

"No," Sumo groaned, "we'll be stuck at your house all day. Adults talk forever."

"Mom said it won't take long." Casey slung his backpack over his shoulder. "Ready, Little Buddy?"

Ready! Dylan danced in place. *I want to show Mom my jersey.* When Casey hooked his leash to his collar, Dylan charged forward.

Casey didn't.

Hey! Dylan looked over his shoulder at Casey. *Are you coming?*

Casey jiggled Dylan's leash. "You know the rules. Walk on my left side and no tugging on the leash."

Yeah, yeah. Dylan moved to Casey's left side and trotted along on the sidewalk.

People juggling umbrellas and picnic baskets walked by and smiled. "Look at that cute dog."

There's a dog? Dylan searched the playground and grassy hills of Carbon Canyon Park. *Where?*

Casey and Dylan waited while a mom and dad helped their little boy on a bicycle go by. The boy let go of a handlebar to point at Dylan and his bike wobbled. His mom caught it in time. "That's Dylan."

"Dylan is the Brea Wildcats' mascot," his dad added.

Dylan gave them a canine grin. *That's me!*

When Casey reached their bike, he unzipped the screen on Dylan's bike trailer.

"Who is this mystery guy?" Sumo got on his bike and reached for his helmet.

"You watch too much TV. No mystery guy." Casey shrugged. "Just some guy."

"I bet it's Cranky Pants," Sumo grumbled, "and your mom was afraid to tell us." He angled into his bike helmet. "If he's there I'm going home."

"Nuh-uh. Mom had a Zoom meeting with him this morning. Besides, he never leaves Beverly Hills."

"That old guy has the dumbest ideas for books."

"Yeah, but Cranston Pantswick is the largest children's book publisher in North America. That's great for my mom's book business because he uses her writers and illustrators a lot."

Sumo made a face. "Remember when he wrote a book about the dog he had as a kid?"

"*Scotch Tape* became a bestseller."

"So what? When he couldn't find a kid to model for the cover of his book," Sumo hooked the helmet strap under his chin, "your mom made me dress up in a stupid sweater and stupid shoes."

I look just like Scotch Tape. Dylan sighed happily. *I got to be on the cover too.*

"She should've made you do it," Sumo grumbled.

"I'm too tall. You're short, skinny and look like him when he was a kid."

"Do not."

"Do too." Casey motioned Dylan inside the bike trailer. "Hop in."

Dylan did and circled twice on his cushion before plopping down. *Not enough time for a world-class snooze before we get home.* He put his muzzle on his front paws. *Just enough time to rest my eyes.*

"Anyway," Casey swung his leg over his bike and pushed off, "we'll be home in five minutes. We'll find out who the guy is."

When Dylan felt the bike turn left and start to go up a hill, he pushed his nose against the side screen of his trailer and sucked in familiar smells. *Almost home.* A breeze blew in barbecue smells from somewhere and Dylan whined. *I love summer.*

Casey's bike made another turn, went up their driveway and stopped. Dylan scratched at the screen of the bike trailer. *Hurry up. I want to show Mom my jersey.*

"Sweet," Sumo gasped.

Casey whispered, "Check it out."

What? Dylan tried for a better look. *All I see is your feet in flip-flops.* He scratched harder on the screen. *Let me out.*

"You gotta see the," Casey unzipped Dylan's screen, "Harley."

Dylan looked around the driveway. *Where's Harley?*

"Not just any Harley." Sumo was into Google, both thumbs working the screen like crazy. "This is a Low Rider ST bike and costs," Sumo's eyes bugged out, "more than some cars."

"I've never seen anything like it." Casey trailed his long fingers over its black shiny finish.

I can see myself. Dylan brought his face closer to the bike. *Are my ears really that fluffy?*

"Dude," Sumo smacked Casey's hand away, "you're getting fingerprints all over it."

"Relax." Casey used the hem of his T-shirt to wipe his prints off, leaving a long smear in their place.

That's worse.

Sumo read some more. "This little baby weighs almost seven hundred pounds." Sumo looked at Casey. "You know someone who rides?"

Casey laughed. "Not Cranky Pants. The guy is seventy-five."

"Let's find out," Casey and Sumo said together.

They raced up the brick walkway, but Dylan beat them. He stretched up on his hind legs and planted his front paws on their door. *Arf!*

"Down, Dylan." Casey pushed the door open. "Mom?"

"Outside on the deck," she called back.

They heard Mom laugh and then a man's low voice. Mom laughed again.

Dylan raced out the open door leading to the deck. He skidded to a stop and studied the tall thin man in a T-shirt, faded blue jeans and scuffed boots. *You're not Cranky Pants.* The man's thumbs were hooked into the front pockets of his jeans. His jet-black hair was pulled straight back and into a short tail. Dylan waggled his butt. *I got a short tail too.*

"Dad!" Sumo ran forward and threw both arms around him.

Dad?

Casey gave him a huge grin. "Hi, Tenn!"

Ten? I can count to ten. Dylan glanced around the deck. *There is only one man here.*

"Mr. Stillwater," Mom corrected and stood up.

"Hi, Casey." Tenn hugged Sumo and then gestured to Dylan. "Is this little guy Dylan? Sumo told me all about him."

"Yeah." Casey scooped Dylan up and held him out. "Dylan was a present from my brother Aiden. Dylan does agility and we've been learning American Sign Language."

Dylan sent Tenn a forty-two teeth grin. *Hi!*

"Great dog." Tenn gave Dylan's topknot a friendly pat. "How was the game?"

"Brea Wildcats won," Casey said.

Arf! Dylan puffed out his chest and waited. *Do you notice anything?*

"Dylan is their mascot," Casey added.

"I see that." Mom smiled and ran a slender hand over the blue and gold lettering. "I like your jersey."

Me too.

"Tenn is really famous," Casey told Dylan. "He played basketball for the Lakers."

That's nice. What are Lakers?

"Mr. Stillwater," Mom repeated.

Tenn gave her a friendly grin. "Lighten up Colleen."

Mom flushed as red as her hair, but she rolled eyes. "At least say Tennyson."

"No way." Tenn placed a hand over his heart and shuddered. "I'm still scarred from being called that as a kid."

"Poor you," Mom teased.

"You try being the only Native American in school named after an English poet." Tenn made a face. "All the other boys had names like Trevor, Justin, and Miles."

"Well, your mother did teach poetry at Cypress College and Lord Tennyson was her favorite poet." Mom tipped her head. "You might have done worse. She could have named you after Percy Bysshe Shelley."

Yikes.

"It's so cool you're here." Sumo beamed up at his dad. "You didn't say you were coming when you called yesterday."

"Well," he began.

Mom took over. "Your dad wants you and Casey to spend a few days at his ranch in Lake Arrowhead."

Why is Tenn's ranch in a lake?

"Get out!" Casey turned Dylan to face him. "Tenn Hundred Acres is the best horse ranch in Lake Arrowhead. The lake is on top of a mountain in the San Bernardino National Forest. Lots of trees and all kinds of animals. We can go hiking and," he broke off and looked to Tenn. "Dylan can go too, right?"

I want to see the ranch in the lake. Whine.

"Sure. The three of you are Dylan's Dog Squad."

We're a team.

"Road trip!" Casey and Sumo whooped.

"Dylan's Dog Squad has like four thousand fans. Wait until I tell them." Sumo brought his cell phone out of his pocket and grinned happily. "Social media is my life."

Casey chimed in. "So far, we've solved every case. Dylan has a great nose. He can find anyone or anything."

Tenn nodded. "Pretty impressive, Dylan."

Arf! I like helping people.

"Oh, wait." Sumo's happy face disappeared. "I can't go." He chewed on his lower lip. "Mom is in Paso Robles."

"That's right." Tenn sucked in a breath. "I forgot. Selena got married again. Who is it this time?"

"Mitchell somebody."

Mom shook her head. "Michael Winters."

"Whatever." Sumo hitched a shoulder and let it fall. "He owns a winery in Paso Robles and has tons of money. Anyway, they're coming home today."

"Actually," Mom began, "your mother called while you were at the game. She and Michael went to Italy on an emergency trip."

"Is everything okay?" Sumo stepped closer. "What kind of emergency, Ms. D?"

"They needed," Mom said slowly, "to pick out a fountain for the villa they're building in Paso Robles."

"Oh." Sumo's voice went flat. "I get it. She's too busy to come home so she sent Dad."

Dylan whined. *Poor kid.*

"No," Tenn disagreed. "I'm here so you can have fun and hang out with me on the ranch. Do guy stuff. It'll be a blast."

"Yeah." Casey punched Sumo on the arm. "Totally awesome. We'll go on trail rides. We'll stay up late at night. Sit around campfires. Tell ghost stories. Eat junk food."

I like junk food.

Sumo perked up. "Is Mrs. Hudson still the cook?"

"You bet." Tenn laughed. "If Mrs. Hudson left, all the ranch hands would leave too. We can't do without her."

"Tenn was telling me about the improvements he's made to the ranch. They sound wonderful." Mom sighed. "I wish I were going with you."

"You're always welcome," Tenn said.

"Dad!" Sumo gaped. "You told Ms. D about the improvements, but you wouldn't tell me. How come?"

"I wanted you to see everything for yourself." Tenn waited a beat but gave in. "I'm excited for you to see the new stable. You'll have your own horses to ride while you're on the ranch."

Sumo brightened. "Really?"

"What about Dylan?" Casey shifted him in his arms. "He's a little guy. He can't go on trail rides."

Dylan leaned against Casey. *Don't leave me home. I want to do guy stuff. Whine.*

"Hmm." Tenn gave Dylan the once over. "He's too big to put in a saddle bag. We could try putting him on a horse."

Alone? No! I'd be too scared.

"Dylan could ride on my lap."

"Not enough room." Tenn thought for a minute. "We can work something out."

Dylan snuffled Casey's cheek. *Yay! I get to go.*

"Are we leaving now? How are we going to get there?" Sumo grinned suddenly. "I could ride on your bike."

"When you're older." Tenn put up both hands to stop an argument. "Besides, I just got the Harley and I'm still getting used to it." He turned to Mom. "Bud Tompkins is parting with his new truck and horse trailer, but they won't be ready until late tonight."

Mom's eyebrows shot up. "He bought them last week. How did you talk him into it?"

Tenn flashed her a grin. "Guess it was my lucky day."

"The boys will need time to pack," Mom mused. "What about eight o'clock tomorrow morning?"

"Sure."

"This stinks," Sumo griped. "Why can't we go now, Ms. D?"

Mom sighed. "Did you forget about Jake?"

"Jake?" Sumo and Casey repeated.

"You're meeting him at Big Belly's for pizza."

Casey slid a look Sumo's way. "Uh."

"Your mom is psychic," Sumo whispered.

"No kidding," Casey whispered back.

"Hardly." Mom gave them a patient smile. "The Brea Wildcats won their game, Jake isn't here," Mom winked at Dylan, "Dylan is their mascot and you boys are always hungry."

Mom is pretty smart.

"Moms know everything," Tenn said. "It's their job. Besides, when I played for the Brea Wildcats, we always went to Big Belly's after every game." Tenn gave Mom a nod. "See you tomorrow morning." He stopped at the door and looked back at Sumo and Casey. "I almost forgot. I have a surprise for you."

TWO

"My dad's here, Ms. D!" Sumo called from the front door.

"Hurry up, Mom. Come on, Dylan!"

Casey, Dylan, and Sumo raced out of the house and down the driveway. The boys dropped their backpacks on the ground next to their bikes and watched Tenn's truck and horse trailer slowly inch its way up the steep hill.

That is a really big horse trailer. Dylan blinked when bright California morning sun glinted off the silver trailer. *And shiny.* Dylan scrambled behind Casey's legs and peeked out. When Tenn eased the truck to the curb and cut its engine, the trailer rocked. *That's strange.*

Tenn hopped out and slammed the truck door. "This is quite the welcoming committee."

Sumo grinned. "We were watching for you."

Tenn gestured to their backpacks. "All set?"

The trailer rocked again, and a loud snort and a quick whinny came from inside. Dylan pawed Casey's leg. *What's going on?*

Sumo's eyes went wide. "Is that our surprise?"

"Could be," Tenn teased.

Casey picked Dylan up. "Want to see?"

Dylan flicked his ears. *Maybe.*

"Hold on." Tenn held up his hand like a traffic cop. "Let's wait for your mom."

A loud bang came from inside of the trailer, sending it rocking again. Dylan leaned against Casey's chest. *Maybe not.*

Tenn glanced at the trailer. "Your surprise is getting restless."

"Hi." Mom came down the driveway carrying Dylan's lunchbox, car seat and harness. She set everything on the ground. "You're late."

"Good morning to you, too," Tenn said good naturedly. "Let me show you why."

Casey, Dylan, and Sumo raced to the back of the trailer and waited for Tenn to open it.

"What happened?" Sumo's index finger traced a long narrow scrape on the side of the trailer. "Did you hit something?"

"Not me." Tenn motioned them to move back while he lowered the ramp. "Take a look."

A reddish-brown filly turned her head their way and watched them enter the trailer. She blew air through her nostrils, flattened her ears, and stomped her hooves.

Sumo stepped closer. "Is she okay?"

"Strangers make her nervous. She'll calm down."

Mom smiled. "You got a new horse."

"You could say that." Tenn's mouth twitched and he added, "She's not a horse. She's a filly."

Dylan bumped Casey's chest. *What's a filly?*

"A filly is a young girl horse," Casey whispered.

Oh. Why didn't Tenn say so?

"I know what a filly is," Mom said dryly and then laughed. "I just don't know why you need another horse."

"You're right. I don't need another horse," Tenn's chin went up, "but she needed me." He hooked a thumb over his shoulder toward the filly. "She's a little skittish. I don't want her getting lost, so I took her to Doc Evans this morning to get microchipped."

Casey smoothed Dylan's topknot out of his eyes. "Dylan is microchipped."

I'll never get lost.

"That's good," Tenn agreed. "It's an owner's responsibility to keep their pets and animals safe. Microchipping does that."

"I didn't know horses were microchipped," Mom said. "I thought they were tattooed under their upper lip."

"If thoroughbred horses are going to race in America," Sumo used two fingers to pull his lip up to show Dylan, "they get a tattoo here."

Interesting. Dylan looked down his muzzle, stuck out his top lip, and tried to see under it. His muzzle quivered and his eyes crossed. *Can't.*

Sumo's fingers let go. "The tattoo for thoroughbreds begins with a letter and that tells the year the horse was born. Then there is a number. If the horse is over twenty-five years old the number is four digits. Younger horses have five-digit numbers." His fingers went back inside his mouth. "If the letther ith Z that meanths the horseth wasth born inth 1996th or 2022th."

You're talking funny.

"How do you know this stuff," Casey asked.

Sumo let go of his mouth. "I read."

"Microchipping horses is a new thing and better in my opinion. Less stressful on the horse." Tenn took his time, letting the filly watch him come closer. "Easy girl." When he reached her side, he ran his hand slowly down her mane and over her flank. "This is Nell. She's a one-year-old sorrel, so she's a yearling."

When she is two will she be a twoling?

"Here you go." Tenn offered her a treat in his open palm. Nell drew back her lips and the treat disappeared.

Nell has really big teeth.

"I'm betting someday she'll be a great quarter horse."

Mom laughed. "Are you playing the ponies now?"

Nell looks too big to play with. Whine.

"Mom wants to know if Tenn is betting on horse races," Casey whispered to Dylan.

Oh. Why didn't she say so?

Tenn held up both hands in surrender. "I'm a horse rancher not a gambler. Just a friendly game of cards now and then. Right, Nell?"

Nell nuzzled his hand and fixed her big dark eyes on him.

"That's enough treats for you."

She disagreed, throwing her head up and nickering.

Dylan gave Nell a tongue-hanging-out-of-his mouth grin. *I like treats too.*

"What are the brown square treats?" Sumo asked. "I thought horses liked apples, carrots, or peppermints."

"Horses will eat all that," Tenn agreed, "but they really like alfalfa and molasses treats. The treats are small, and I use them for training." He ran a hand over her flank. "I don't want a fat horse."

"Can I touch her?" Sumo started toward her.

Nell thought not and her dark brown eyes flashed. She tossed her head back, let out a high whinny and backed away.

"Wait Sumo." Tenn placed an arm around Nell's shoulder, brought his face down to hers and soothed, "Easy, girl. Easy."

"Sorry." Sumo stood still. "Didn't mean to spook her."

Nell snorted and showed her teeth.

Don't be afraid. It will be okay. Dylan let out a slow whine.

Nell swung her head, following Dylan's whine. Her eyes calmed when they reached him. She let out another whinny, this time soft and low.

"Hey, I thought you were *my girl*," Tenn joked and scratched her muzzle. "Do you like Dylan?"

Nell kept her eyes on Dylan, but she bumped her head lightly against Tenn's chest.

Casey shifted Dylan in his arms. "What's going on?"

Tenn laughed. "I think Nell has a new friend. Has Dylan ever seen a horse before?"

"Our friends have Arabians. Dylan has seen them ride the horses," Mom said, "but he hasn't seen a horse up close."

Horses look like tall dogs. Dylan looked at his fluffy paws. *They have big feet like me but they're not fluffy.*

"Bring Dylan closer."

"Dylan," Casey hugged him, "want to say hi to Nell?"

Arf!

Mom, Tenn, and Sumo laughed.

"I meant do you want to touch her?"

Oh. Dylan turned his head away. *It wasn't that funny.*

"Over here Dylan." Sumo was still laughing but he had his cell phone up, recording a video. "Wait until Dylan's Dog Squad fans see you with your new friend. We'll get a thousand hits."

Casey placed Dylan's front paw between Nell's ears

and gently ran it down her forelock. "They like to be stroked."

Your hair is rough. My hair is fluffy and soft.

Nell kept her eyes on Dylan and swished her long tail.

I wish I had a long tail. Dylan sighed and waggled his short tail instead.

"What are you going to do with this big trailer?" Mom gestured to the other three stalls.

"Since it can hold four horses, it will be great for traveling to horse events." Tenn pointed to the last stall. "Today it will haul my Harley and the boys' bikes up to the ranch. See the door beyond the last stall? That leads to the living quarters."

"Really?" Sumo angled his head for a better look.

"It has a kitchen, bedroom, living area and bathroom. This trailer has everything, even air conditioning. Much better than fans for the horses," he gave a quick laugh, "and for me."

"This is awesome." Sumo moved to the side wall of the trailer, dropped a window, stood on tiptoes, and leaned out. "You can hang baskets of hay on the outside. The horses can look out and eat while you're driving."

What a good idea. Dylan nudged Casey. *Hint, hint.*

"You just had breakfast," Casey said. "It's too early for treats."

Nell got a treat.

"We need to get going, boys." Tenn leaned in close to Nell and whispered, "It's going to be okay. You'll be home soon."

Nell blew out her nostrils and backed up.

"Boys, grab your gear and get in the truck," Tenn said. "I need to load your bikes up."

"Road trip! I'm calling shotgun." Sumo ran ahead.

When Casey, Dylan and Mom reached the truck, Sumo was already slouched in the passenger seat, his flip-flops off and both feet on the dashboard.

"Sumo." Mom gave him The Look.

"Sorry, Ms. D." Sumo's feet slid off and he sat up.

Casey opened the back door and put Dylan on the seat. "Look out my window. I need to get your car seat and harness set up."

Dylan walked across the back seat. *Your window is closed.* He brought his nose to the window and snuffled across the glass, trying for smells. *Nope.* He huffed out a breath and the window fogged a little. *Interesting.* Dylan ran his nose over the fog, leaving a trail. *My first road trip. Arf!* He came back to Casey and wagged his butt. *I'm excited.*

"Hold on." Casey threw their backpacks on the floor.

Dylan went back to the window and scratched at the glass. *Tenn should've left the window down.* Dylan got on his hind legs, planted his front paws on the back of the driver's seat and stretched forward. *Tenn's window is down. Nice.* Dylan raised his snout and sucked in smells. *Home smells so good. I'm going to miss these smells.*

"Here you go, Little Buddy." Casey patted Dylan's car seat and waited until Dylan climbed into it. "Lift your muzzle up." Casey brought the harness across Dylan's chest.

Too tight. Grr.

Casey ran his hand under the harness and adjusted it. "Better?"

Dylan slurped a quick canine kiss on Casey's cheek. *Ready!*

"We're going to have a blast on the ranch." Casey ran

around to the other side of the truck and climbed in. "Dylan! You got snot and slobber all over my window."

Did not. Dylan ignored Casey when he pointed to the streaks covering his window. *Maybe just a little.*

Casey leaned forward and tapped Sumo on the shoulder. "Want to give us your backpack? We've got room on the floor."

"Yeah." Sumo handed it over.

Casey turned to Dylan and put a finger to his lips, signing Quiet.

Dylan watched Casey take a T-shirt out of Sumo's backpack and wipe the nose prints and slobber off the window. Then he shoved the shirt into the backpack and grinned at Dylan.

Oh brother.

Tenn opened the driver's door and slid in. "Are you sure you've got everything?"

"Yeah," Casey and Sumo said.

"Let's go."

"Not so fast." Mom held up Dylan's lunchbox. She gestured for Casey to lower his window and handed it to him. "I've packed Dylan's lunch."

Yum. Dylan's nose quivered. *Roast beef.*

"Colleen," Tenn made a face, "I do have food on the ranch."

"I know. I've spoken to Mrs. Hudson and explained Dylan is on a low-fat diet. She's okay with fixing his meals."

Thanks Mom.

"It only takes ninety minutes to get to the ranch." Tenn snorted. "We'll be there before lunchtime."

"Yes," Mom tipped her head. "This is for when you stop at McDonald's in San Bernardino."

Dylan whipped his head around. *Who told you?*

Mom cupped Dylan's muzzle in her hands. "You can't have hamburgers. Too much fat isn't good for you."

Aw Mom. We're going on a road trip. All the guys are getting hamburgers at McDonald's. I don't want to be left out.

Tenn tried for an innocent face. "Who says we're stopping at McDonald's?"

"Tennyson Stillwater," Mom cut him off, "everyone knows everyone always stops at the McDonald's in San Bernardino before going up the mountain to Lake Arrowhead."

Dylan sighed. *Mom is pretty smart.*

Just then a siren wailed, and they all turned to see a police car speeding down Carbon Canyon Highway.

Two more police cars followed with sirens and lights flashing.

"Wow! Three cop cars, Ms. D."

"What's going on, Mom?"

"Something must have happened in Chino Hills," she murmured.

"Probably an accident." Tenn's voice was casual. "Is Rory still a cop?"

"My big brother is now Detective Lieutenant," Mom said proudly.

Uncle Rory catches bad guys.

"That's great." Tenn nodded. "Tell him to call me sometime. We have a lot to catch up on."

Mom stepped back from the truck and waved. "Have a great time."

Casey lifted Dylan's paw. "Say goodbye to Mom."

Arf!

"Bye Ms. D!"

Tenn guided the truck and horse trailer down the hill.

When he got to Carbon Canyon Highway, he put on his right turn signal.

"That's the long way," Sumo groaned. "Go through the canyon. It's shorter."

"Are you taking the long way because of the accident?" Casey checked out the empty stretch of highway. "It seems okay now."

Tenn pulled onto the highway. "I don't want to drive by Bud Tompkins' ranch. He wasn't too happy about parting with his truck and trailer."

"Why," Sumo pressed. "He sold them to you."

Tenn hesitated. "Can you boys keep a secret?"

Whine.

"A secret is something someone tells you about someone or something that you're not supposed to know about," Casey explained, "and you can't tell anyone else."

What came after a secret is something someone tells you?

"I didn't want to say anything in front of your mom." Tenn's eyes met Casey's in the rearview mirror. "I've known her all my life and you know how she gets."

Uh-oh. This isn't good.

Casey leaned forward. "Are you in trouble?"

"Nothing like that."

"You told Ms. D that Mr. Tompkins sold the truck and trailer to you."

"I told her," Tenn said slowly, "Bud Tompkins was *parting* with his new truck and horse trailer."

"You lied to Mom?" Casey's voice shot up. "Are you nuts?"

This is definitely not good.

Tenn kept his eyes on the road. "Not exactly."

"Ms. D says, 'Omission is the most powerful form of a lie'."

"Actually, George Orwell said it," Casey corrected Sumo. "Mom just says it a lot because we mess up a lot."

True.

"So," Sumo wouldn't let it go, "exactly what's the truth?"

"I won the truck and trailer in a blackjack game."

That doesn't sound too bad. What's a blackjack game?

"Okay." Casey took over. "What about Nell?"

"The truck and trailer didn't cover Bud's losses. He threw in the horse, and we cut for the truck, trailer, and horse. Bud drew a three to my jack of spades."

"He lost." Sumo shrugged. "You won fair and square. He's got nothing to be mad about."

"Wait a minute," Casey said, leaning forward again. "Does any of this have to do with the scrape on the trailer?"

"Bud shot at me as I was leaving," Tenn grimaced, "so, yeah, he's mad."

Uh-oh.

THREE

"You're snoring, Little Buddy." Casey gently rubbed Dylan's shoulder. "We're in San Bernardino. Wake up."

Wha? Dylan blinked himself awake.

Sumo hung over the front seat and brought his cell phone close to Dylan's face. "Wait until Dylan's Dog Squad fans see these pictures. You were drooling."

Was not. Dylan snapped his mouth shut and bit his tongue. *Ow! Maybe just a little.* Dylan stretched himself up and into a sitting position. He blinked again and a jaw cracking yawn escaped. *My world class snooze was really good.*

Tenn opened Dylan's door and gave him a quick scratch down his back. "I'm going to fuel up." He pulled cash from his pocket and held it out to Casey. "You can get us a snack at McDonald's."

"I'm starving." Sumo bounced out of the truck and came around. "Road trips make me hungry."

Gotta love Sumo. Everything makes him hungry and he's a slob. Dylan sighed happily. *I'm sitting next to him.*

Casey shook his head. "Mom gave me money. Thanks anyway."

Now Tenn shook his head. "I believe in paying the help."

Huh?

"Dad!" Sumo put both hands on his hips. "You're going to make us work while we're on the ranch? Not fair."

"It is if you want to eat." Tenn handed the money to Casey. "I'll have a Quarter Pounder with cheese, French fries and iced tea."

"Okay." Casey grabbed his backpack and Dylan's lunchbox. "We'll meet you on the outdoor patio."

"Sounds good."

"See ya." Sumo took off.

Hurry up! Dylan snuffled Casey's cheek. *Sumo is halfway to the Golden Arches and you're still getting me out of the truck.*

"Stay still. You've got your Dylan's Dog Squad bandana all bunched up." Casey smoothed it out. "There."

I love my bandana. Dylan nuzzled it. *Thanks.*

Casey unbuckled Dylan's harness, clipped his leash to his collar, and tucked him under his arm. "You're as bad as Sumo when it comes to food."

Am not. Dylan caught the smells of fast food and he wiggled to be put down. *Maybe just a little.*

"I'm carrying you. The asphalt is too hot for you to walk on. You'll burn your paws."

Walk fast.

Casey and Dylan joined Sumo behind a red Mini Cooper in the drive thru lane. When it was their turn, Casey stepped up to the window.

The window slid open. "Hello and welcome to McDonald's. I'm Mario. What are you hungry for?"

Arf! Dylan swung his head toward Casey. *I like this place.*

"Everything," Sumo said.

Mario glared at Sumo then Casey and then Dylan. "You got no car." He slammed the window shut.

You got no manners. Grr.

"Open up." Casey banged once on the glass and pointed to where Tenn was fueling the truck. "Our ride is over there."

Mario slid the window back two inches. "This is a drive thru. You're not driving through."

So what? Dylan stomach rumbled and he pawed the air. *We're on a road trip and we're hungry.*

Sumo muscled Casey out of the way and used both hands to slide the window back. "Our ride wouldn't fit in your drive thru lane."

"Not my problem." Mario stood tall.

"Look," Casey began, "you sell fast food." He put money on the counter. "We're here to buy fast food."

The car parade behind them agreed and drivers honked their horns.

"Fast food is supposed to be fast," Sumo insisted. "We could've been out of here by now."

An older guy with a skinny moustache and wearing a white starched shirt nudged Mario aside. "I'm Vincent, the manager. Is there a problem?"

Mario declared, "There's a *dog* in the drive thru."

A dog? Dylan looked around. *Where?*

Sumo spoke up. "Mario won't take our order."

"This is Dylan's first road trip," Casey brought Dylan closer to the window, "and I promised him we'd get McDonald's."

"They don't have a car." Mario's mouth set in a thin line. "No car. No chow."

Say it isn't so, Casey. I want chow. Whine.

Vincent started to speak. Then he snapped his fingers and a smile spread over his face. "I know you. You're Dylan." He brought out his cell phone. "I'm a Dylan's Dog Squad fan. I follow you on social media. You do search and rescue." He showed Dylan's picture to Mario.

Mario ignored it. "No car. No chow."

Vincent was on a roll. "I remember when you found the little boy at the mall and when you caught The Sledgehammer."

Sumo beamed. "Thanks to Dylan, The Sledgehammer is now in jail."

"Good boy!" Vincent gave Dylan a friendly pat. "Mario, give our heroes anything they want. Today they're eating on the house."

"But!"

Dylan leaned against Casey. *I thought we were eating on the patio.*

"Anything they want." Vincent nailed Mario with a look. "And be quick about it."

Mario waited for Vincent to walk away before he sneered, "Happy?"

Arf!

"I'll have a Big Mac, French fries and vanilla milkshake," Casey said.

What about me? Dylan's ears drooped.

"We'll share the milkshake, Little Buddy."

Okay.

"Also," Casey pointed to Tenn still fueling up at the gas pump, "he'll have a Quarter Pounder with cheese, French fries and iced tea."

The car behind them honked its horn.

"Is that all?"

"I want two Big Macs, two French fries, extra ketchup, chocolate shake—make that two chocolate shakes, chocolate chip cookies and two apple pies." Sumo smiled. "Apples are good for me."

Mario relayed their order to the kitchen and slammed the window shut.

How long does it take to get fast food? Dylan squirmed under the bright sun. *It's hot out here.* He brought his face close to Casey's and panted. *Really hot.*

"We're getting a table, Sumo. Dylan needs water."

The driver behind them laid on his horn again and leaned out the car window. "What about fast food you don't understand?"

"Go on. I got this." Sumo rapped on the glass. "Mario! We're starving out here."

The patio was crowded with parents and kids. Their tables were littered with drinks, food waiting to be devoured and paper wrappers. At one table two kids were fighting over the last Chicken McNugget. Dylan wrinkled his nose and inhaled deeply. *I love the smell of grease and fast food.*

Casey found a table with an umbrella. He put Dylan on the bench, unhooked his leash and stuffed it into his pocket. "It's too hot for you to sit on the ground."

Fine by me. Dylan scooted closer to the table. *I'll be able to see what everyone is eating.* Dylan checked out the table next to him. Teenagers were laughing and working their way through stacks of Big Macs and piles of French fries. *I wish I had a Big Mac.*

Casey got a bottle of water from his backpack and filled Dylan's collapsible dish. "Here."

Dylan sniffed once, turned up his snout and looked away. *Warm.*

Casey took out his cell phone. "I'll tell Sumo to get a cup of ice."

Thanks. Dylan nose bumped his lunchbox. *Hint, hint.*

"Okay," Casey unpacked Dylan's dish and filled it with roast beef, "but wait until Sumo and Tenn get here." He zipped up Dylan's lunchbox and put it aside.

Dylan got closer, inhaled the smell of roast beef, and licked his lips. *Yum.*

"What do you like best about the road trip?"

Gee, tough call. I've had a world class snooze and now I'm having a snack. Dylan sent a look Casey's way. *Both.*

"Do you see the San Bernardino mountains?"

Dylan studied the sprawling mountains in the distance. *They're really big.*

"In the winter they're covered in snow. We can visit Tenn and go sledding. You'll like that."

Awesome. What's sledding?

Dylan saw Tenn pull the truck and trailer to a side parking lot filled with RVs, campers, and other horse trailers. Then he climbed out and went over to Sumo. After a minute Tenn and Sumo started walking toward them juggling bags of food and drinks.

"Here they come, Little Buddy." Casey raised his hand and waved them over.

Keep watching Sumo and Tenn. Don't look at me. Dylan tucked his buns under him, leaned forward and slowly stretched his muzzle toward the roast beef.

"Hey!" Casey clamped Dylan's muzzle shut with one hand and pushed the dish away from him with his other hand. "You can wait."

No, I can't. Dylan shook himself free.

"Here." Sumo put the cup of ice in front of Casey. He dropped onto the bench beside Dylan and looked inside the bags of food before passing one over. "This is yours."

"Thanks." Casey added ice to Dylan's water dish. "Okay. Now it's chow time."

About time. Dylan polished off his snack while Casey was still unwrapping his. *Whine.*

"I heard you." Casey took a bite of his Big Mac and offered Dylan a French fry. "Eat slow. You don't want to puke in the truck."

I never puke. Dylan gulped down the French fry and pawed the table. *More.*

"Casey's right." Tenn drank some iced tea. "The mountain road has a lot of curves and switchbacks. I'll go slow because of the trailer, but you'll want to take it easy on the food."

"That's why I'm eating light." Sumo mumbled through a mouthful of French fries.

Dylan checked out Sumo's snack. *Your food covers half the table, and everything is drowned in ketchup.* Dylan sidled his buns closer to Sumo. *Need help with anything?*

Sumo swallowed, reached for his chocolate shake with his left hand and picked up his apple pie with his right. A chunk of pie broke off.

Dylan shot out his long pink tongue and caught the pie midair. *Yum. I love apples.* Dylan scooted back to Casey. He hooked his muzzle over Casey's arm and stared at the milkshake. *You promised we'd share.*

Casey helped himself to more French fries. "What are we doing when we get to the ranch?"

"I want to get Nell settled first." Tenn wiped his mouth with a paper napkin. "I checked on her while I was getting fuel. She's taking the trip well but going up the mountain might be hard on her."

"What's the big deal?" Sumo asked. "She's in a fancy horse trailer."

"Traveling amounts to sensory contradiction for horses."

Sensory what? Dylan nudged Casey.

Casey held both hands palms up. "Dunno."

"When a horse is standing still but is feeling movement," Tenn explained, "they can get motion sickness. Kind of like when people get car sickness. The problem is horses can't vomit."

No problem. Dylan sneaked a French fry from Casey's lunch. *Don't give her any French fries.*

Casey moved the fries away from Dylan. "Are you serious about racing Nell?"

"I am."

"What if she can't race?" Sumo started on the chocolate chip cookies.

Tenn shrugged. "Then she'll have a happy life on the ranch."

Sumo chewed his cookie. "You won't sell her?"

"I'd never sell or give up an animal or pet." Tenn gave a slight shake of his head. "It wouldn't be right. They trust you to take care of them."

You're a nice man.

"Mr. Tompkins gave up Nell." Sumo went after another cookie. "He could've borrowed the money to pay you back."

"I'm guessing he couldn't. Bud went into debt to add a new well on his ranch just before Covid hit. Those were hard times for everyone."

"You made a lot of improvements on the ranch. Are you doing okay?"

"I've been lucky all my life. When I played for the

Lakers, I made a lot of money. My dream was always to buy a ranch. I invested my money and one day my dream came true."

"You weren't lucky," Sumo argued. "You worked hard."

"I'm grateful for what I have." Tenn put both elbows on the table. "Now it's time for me to give back." He toyed with his empty iced tea container. "I'm turning part of Tenn Hundred Acres into a sports ranch. A place where kids can learn to ride, care for horses, and play ball."

Casey perked up. "What kind of ball?"

Tenn laughed. "Basketball, of course. I just finished the new basketball court. That's one of the improvements I was telling your mom about."

"Oh," Casey and Sumo said flatly.

"Now I'm going to get started on the baseball field."

Casey and Sumo fist bumped. "Yes!"

Casey, Sumo, and I play ball. Dylan thought about the Brea Wildcats. *Maybe I could be your mascot. Then I'll have two jerseys.*

"To do it right will be a lot of work." Tenn rubbed his hands together happily. "I can't wait."

"Sounds great," Casey said. "We could help you."

Tenn gave them a slow grin. "I'm counting on it."

"You and your big fat mouth," Sumo grumbled. "Now we'll be stuck doing work. This trip is supposed to be fun."

"It'll be fun. Dylan's never been on a horse ranch." Casey tossed out the last of the water in Dylan's collapsible dish and poured in vanilla milkshake. "Here you go."

That's it? Dylan sniffed at the tiny puddle of milkshake and then stared up at Casey. *It barely covers the bottom of my dish. Grr.*

"You just had a snack, and we'll get lunch at the ranch."

Casey finished his Big Mac and grabbed a napkin. "Mrs. Hudson is a great cook."

She'd better be. Dylan gave the milkshake two licks and it disappeared. Then he gave the dish a hard nudge with his nose sending it flying toward Casey.

Casey caught the dish before it landed in his lap. "Hey!"

More milkshake. Dylan started to arf but stopped when he saw a man with dark blond hair running in the side parking lot. *You're carrying something like big scissors with shiny jaws on one end and long wooden handles.* Sunlight bounced off the shiny jaws. *That's weird.*

The man flattened himself against a white van, crouched and looked around. Then he crept to the back of Tenn's trailer. When he got to the trailer ramp, he looked around again.

Something is wrong. Dylan stretched up to get a better look. He saw the man heft the big scissors and use the jaws to grab the lock on the trailer. The man forced the handles together and the lock broke off. *No! The trailer doesn't belong to you!* Dylan's paws danced on the bench. *Arf! Arf!*

"Settle down," Casey grabbed Dylan's shoulders. "You're not getting any more milkshake."

There's a bad guy at the trailer! Dylan leaped over Casey. *Arf! Arf!* Dylan hit the ground and stumbled. He shook his ears out of eyes and ran. *Arf! Follow me.*

Casey sprang to his feet. "Dylan needs help!"

Tenn got up. "How do you know?"

"I just know! C'mon, Sumo!"

Sumo got up. "Where's Dylan going?"

Dylan ran straight for Bad Guy, his paws eating up the parking lot. *Grr!*

A delivery truck swung into the parking lot. Its

windows were down, music was blaring out and the driver was singing along.

Dylan's heart banged in his chest when he saw Bad Guy toss the big scissors away and reach for the latch. *You're not going to steal Nell. I won't let you.* Dylan kept his eyes on Bad Guy and picked up the pace.

"No!" someone screamed.

"That little dog is going to get hit!"

"Help! Somebody help!"

Dylan saw a blur of tires. Then he heard the screech of brakes.

FOUR

Yip!

The truck's front tire clipped Dylan's hip and sent him rolling under the truck.

Watch where you're going!

The crowd in the parking lot turned to look.

"Hey, you!"

"Stop the truck!"

"You hit a dog!"

"Somebody get help!"

The truck slammed on its brakes. The smell of burning rubber filled the air. Everyone ran to the truck, got down on hands and knees and looked. Helping hands reached under the truck.

"Come here, little fella."

"Don't be scared."

"He's in shock."

"Somebody get a blanket."

Ohhh. Pain arrowed through Dylan, and he groaned. *This isn't good.* Dylan's eyes fluttered open. He stared into the kind faces of strangers backlit by bright sun. Dust swirled like big halos around their heads. *Am I dead?* He tummy crawled from under the truck and scrambled to his paws. *Whine.*

"Daddy, the dog is hurt." A little girl started to cry. "Help him!"

"We will, honey." He wrapped his arms around her and held her close.

"Dylan!" Casey called and pushed his way through. "I'm coming!"

Where are you? Dylan let out a long low whine and struggled to see past the faces. *Do you see me?* Dylan tried a full body wag. *Ow! That hurt.*

A woman held out both hands in front of her and slowly got down to his level. "There, there," she soothed. Gently she ran her hands over him. "Stay still. You may have broken something."

"I'm sorry." The truck driver knelt beside Dylan. "I didn't see you." He reached for Dylan's collar. "Are you lost?"

No. I'm chasing a bad guy. Dylan looked around the truck driver and saw Bad Guy lowering the ramp on Tenn's truck. *He's stealing Nell!* Dylan searched the faces in the crowd and saw Casey, Sumo, and Tenn break through. *About time you got here.* Dylan gave the truck driver's hand a quick lick. *Thanks! I feel better. Gotta go!*

Dylan ran toward Tenn's trailer, his paws skimming the ground. When he reached the trailer, he was panting hard. Keeping his eyes on Bad Guy, he slowed to catch his breath and padded closer.

"Easy does it," Bad Guy muttered to himself. Balancing the ramp with both hands, he brought it to his knees.

No, you don't! Dylan gave it all he had and leaped, hitting the man in the small of his back.

"Hey!" Bad Guy lost his grip and fell face first onto the ramp.

Dylan jumped on him. *Grr! Grr!*

Inside the trailer Nell whinnied and kicked. Somewhere sirens sounded, coming closer and louder.

"Dylan," Casey ran up, waving his arms, "get away from him!"

Tenn and Sumo circled Dylan and Bad Guy.

"Casey's right," Tenn said. "Wait for the sheriff."

No.

Bad Guy was on his hands and knees, struggling to get up.

Dylan went after him again. *You're not getting away.* Dylan clamped his jaws around Bad Guy's worn cowboy boots. *Yeck!* He shot his tongue in and out. *Your boots are dirty and taste awful.*

Bad Guy kicked out and his boot caught Dylan on the side of the head.

That really hurt!

"Somebody get this mutt off me!" Bad Guy rolled onto his back and kicked out with both feet.

Dylan came back for more. *I'm not a mutt. I'm an American Cocker Spaniel.* He sprang, making a four-paw landing on Bad Guy's chest. Getting in close Dylan got a mouthful of his shirt and shook it.

Bad Guy grabbed Dylan's collar with one hand and twisted. "I'll teach you!"

"Little Buddy." Casey pulled Dylan's leash from his pocket and made a lasso out of it. "Get down." Casey sailed the lasso neatly around Bad Guy's free hand.

"You little snot!" Bad Guy snarled. "Wait 'til I get ahold of you and your dumb mutt!"

I'm not dumb but you are. Dylan pounced on Bad Guy

again and growled in his face. *You can't talk to Casey that way. Grr.*

Casey gave the leash one quick jerk and held on. "Don't even think about it."

A sheriff's SUV raced in from the main parking lot, spitting up gravel and dust. Two female deputies got out, slammed their doors, and came their way. One deputy was in uniform. The other deputy was wearing jeans and a cotton shirt. Both deputies had their hands resting on their guns. Looky-loos from the McDonald's patio picked up their Happy Meals and drinks and came too.

"People," one deputy faced the crowd, stopping them in their tracks, "go back to your tables. Mind your own business. Let us do our job."

The onlookers waited until the deputies turned around before they hustled along behind them. This was too good to miss.

Dylan studied the women. *You must be like the police. You have guns like Uncle Rory.* Dylan wagged his short tail and gave them a happy grin. *I like your badges.* Dylan sighed. *I wish I had one.*

"I'm Detective Melodia and this is Deputy Ito." Detective Melodia's gaze shifted to Bad Guy on the ground. "Somebody want to tell me what's going on?"

"Give it up, Dude," Sumo said to Bad Guy. "Spill your guts."

"Dunno what you're talking about," he mumbled.

"I'm the one who called." Tenn cleared his throat. "I'm Tennyson Stillwater. This is my son Sumo Modragon and his best friend Casey Donovan."

Arf! What about me?

"That's Dylan. He saw this guy breaking into Tenn's

trailer." Casey gave Dylan's leash a hard yank, making Bad Guy's right hand come up in a clumsy wave.

"Hey," Bad Guy protested and rubbed his leashed wrist with his free hand. "Not me."

Casey went on, "Dylan stopped him from stealing Tenn's horse."

"Horse?" Bad Guy gave his scraggly beard a grubby four finger scratch. "What horse? There ain't no horse."

Kicking came from inside the trailer, sending it rocking.

There's a horse.

"Excuse me," Tenn said to the deputies and brushed past them. "I've got to calm my horse before she hurts herself."

Deputy Ito nodded to Tenn and went back to Bad Guy. "You were saying?"

"Don't know nothin' about no horse. I heard a noise. Thought somebody might be in trouble." Bad Guy sat up straight and gave them a yellow toothed grin. "Just tryin' to be a good citizen."

Deputy Ito doubted it. "You got a name?"

"Me?" Bad Guy went blank and then looked around the parking lot for inspiration. He saw the Golden Arches and his face lit up. "McDonald."

Sumo snorted. "Like in Ronald McDonald?"

"Nah." He shook his head. "Ronny. Only my ma calls me Ronald."

"We need to see some identification," Detective Melodia ordered.

Bad Guy screwed up his face. "I left the house kinda sudden like. Wanted to get me some lunch." He rubbed his belly. "I was real hungry. Ya know?"

"Uh-huh. Show me your money." Deputy Ito pointed to his pockets. "Use your free hand."

"Sure, sure." Bad Guy pulled his pockets inside out. "Whatta ya know? I thought I had money, but I must've forgot it."

"Uh-huh." Deputy Ito walked over to the bolt cutters. "Want to tell me about these?"

Bad Guy's eyes went wide. "I ain't never seen them before. Someone must've dropped them."

Detective Melodia raised her eyebrows and motioned her partner aside. They talked for a minute and then Deputy Ito pulled out an iPad. She tapped on it a few times, looked up and nodded.

Detective Melodia turned aside and spoke into her radio. After a minute, she clicked off. "Congrats!" she announced. "You're on your way to the station."

"Ah now why ya wanna go and do that," Bad Guy complained. "I ain't done nothin'. You got this all wrong."

"Don't think so," Detective Melodia said. "Want to bet we'll find your fingerprints on the bolt cutters, the lock and the truck ramp?"

"That so?" Bad Guy frowned. "I only touched them a little bit."

Wow. Even I know that's a confession and I'm a dog. Dylan sighed. *I almost feel sorry for catching you.*

"Hands behind your back. You're being charged with Burglary, Penal Code 459 and Attempted Grand Theft, Penal Code 487. Depending on how you check out, Ronald McDonald, we might be adding False Identification, Penal Code 148.9."

"Seems like a lot," grumbled Bad Guy. "I wasn't here that long."

Deputy Ito traded Dylan's leash for handcuffs, snapped them on and pulled him to his feet. "You have the right to remain silent."

Detective Melodia said, "Get moving."

"Nuh-uh. I'm not goin' nowhere." He glanced over his shoulder at Deputy Ito. "You left out the part about me gettin' a lawyer. I know my rights."

"How many times have you been arrested? Smile, Ronny." Sumo held his cell phone up. When he caught Detective Melodia's warning look, he shoved it into his pocket.

"As for stealing the horse, you have a pending charge," Detective Melodia informed Ronny. "Grand Theft, Penal Code 487."

"What about Dylan?" Casey picked up Dylan. "That guy kicked him twice."

Dylan leaned against Casey. *It hurt.*

"You're right. Adding two counts of Animal Cruelty, Penal Code 597. Take him away, Deputy Ito."

Onlookers erupted into wild cheers and fist bumping when Deputy Ito marched Ronny, his head down and cowboy boots shuffling, past them. Cell phones and videos got the big moment Deputy Ito put him into the SUV. When she got behind the wheel, the crowd broke up and headed back to MacDonald's. It was time for dessert.

Detective Melodia turned to Casey. "I doubt if our friend acted alone. If I learn he was hired to steal Mr. Stillwater's horse and I can identify who hired him, I'll add Conspiracy to Commit Grand Theft, PC 182 and PC 487."

"You're charging Ronny with a lot," Casey said. "Do you have enough evidence to make it stick?"

Detective Melodia raised her eyebrows.

"My Uncle Rory is a Detective Lieutenant with Brea PD."

"Then you know the drill."

Sumo got excited. "I bet you're going to grill him at the

station. Make him squeal and roll over on the scumbag who hired him."

She shot a look to Casey.

"Sumo watches too much TV."

It sounded like a good idea to me.

"Not to worry." Detective Melodia tried not to smile. "He's in enough trouble right now. He's not going anywhere."

Tenn came down the ramp and over to them.

"How is Nell," Sumo asked.

"She's okay. We'll walk her in a bit." Tenn ruffled Dylan's ears. "Thank you for saving Nell."

Arf! Just doing my job!

"Mr. Stillwater," Detective Melodia blushed, "I remember when you played for the Lakers. I'm a big fan." She smiled. "Why are you in San Bernardino?"

"Dad owns Tenn Hundred Acres Ranch in Lake Arrowhead." Sumo gestured to the mountains. "We're going there now."

"My son Noah and I live in Lake Arrowhead, and he goes to Lake Arrowhead Academy. We pass by your ranch every day when I take him to school. It really looks great. You've made a lot of changes."

"Thanks. It's been hard work," Tenn clapped his hands on Casey's and Sumo's shoulders, "but luckily for me, I'm getting some help for a few days."

"Tell my dad child labor is against the law," Sumo pleaded.

Detective Melodia grinned. "Good luck with that one."

"The best part is," Casey broke in, "Tenn is turning part of the ranch into a sports ranch. Kids will learn how to ride and care for horses."

Sumo punched Casey's arm. "Don't forget about learning to play baseball and basketball."

Don't forget. Dylan pawed the air. *I want to be the mascot.*

"Sounds like a great plan. Speaking of plans," Detective Melodia ran a hand over Dylan's shoulders, "you were very brave to stop Ronny. I'm sure he planned on stealing the horse and being long gone by now."

"Dylan would've found them," Casey bragged. "He's got a great nose. He can find anyone or anything."

Nell is my friend.

"That's amazing. How long have you had Dylan?"

"My brother Aiden sent him to me this summer, but we've already done a lot. Dylan does Agility, has passed the American Kennel Club Canine Good Citizen test, can count to ten and we're learning American Sign Language."

Detective Melodia smiled at Dylan, put her hands in the air and twisted them a couple of times.

Wow! Dylan wiggled his butt. *You signed, Yay!*

"You know sign language," Casey and Sumo said together.

"Noah is eleven years old and hearing impaired. When he was four," Detective Melodia explained, "he had a high fever and suffered a hearing loss. Noah is lucky because he speaks well and reads lips. Other kids aren't so lucky." She smiled. "Why do you know it?"

"Lots of reasons. Dylan's a pup now but dogs sometime lose their hearing when they get older." Casey stroked Dylan's head. "Since Dylan knows sign language, he'll always be able to understand me."

"That's great."

"We're Dylan's Dog Squad," Sumo added. "We do search and rescue."

Dylan wiggled his shoulders. *See my Dylan's Dog Squad bandana?*

"When we're working," Casey added, "sometimes we have to be quiet, or we don't want anyone to know what we're saying."

"We just started the business, but Dylan has solved every case." Sumo pulled out his cell phone and held it up. "I do social media."

"Dylan's Dog Squad has thousands of followers," Tenn said. "Maybe you heard about their latest case. The boys and Dylan were in Oʻahu. Kekoa Ailana came to them for help because healing waters from Sacred Falls were being stolen."

"I remember the story," Detective Melodia said slowly. "It was in the news. Billionaire Howard Fountain was arrested for stealing the healing waters." She shook her head. "He had some crazy idea the waters would keep him alive forever."

Howard kidnapped Casey, Sumo and Kekoa. And he dognapped me. Now he'll be living in prison forever.

"The story also said Casey's mom has a book business and her client is Cranston Pantswick." Detective Melodia suddenly pointed to Dylan and Sumo. "You two are on the cover of his book *Scotch Tape*. That's Noah's favorite book. He's crazy about dogs." She grinned. "Actually, he's crazy about all animals."

"You should bring Noah to the ranch." Casey hugged Dylan. "He can meet Dylan."

Arf!

"That's a great idea." Tenn gestured to the horse trailer. "Noah can also meet Nell and the other horses."

"Thanks. Noah would like that. He's been riding since he was three. My parents have a couple of horses."

Detective Melodia started past Tenn but stopped when she spotted the long gash on the trailer. She ran her hand slowly over it. "Did you hit something?"

"No." Tenn shrugged. "Something must've hit me."

Mr. Tompkins shot at you. Grr.

Casey put his index finger to his lips, signing Quiet.

Why? Mr. Tompkins isn't a nice man.

"I'll call you with an update on the case." Detective Melodia gave Dylan a friendly muzzle rub and them a wave. "Bye."

Dylan squirmed and kicked out with his back paws. *It's hot.*

"Don't wander off." Casey put him down. "I'm going to toss our stuff in Tenn's truck."

Dylan put his nose to the ground and sniffed around the ramp. His head shot up when bumps and snorts came from the trailer, followed by two kicks. *Riding in a horse trailer all day must be boring. Nell needs company.*

Dylan trotted up the ramp but when Nell fixed her eyes on him, he slowed. *Don't be afraid.*

Nell dipped her head and blew through her nostrils.

Dylan went to her stall and plunked his rump down. *All I see are your knees.* He tilted his head back. *That hurts my neck.* Dylan got on his hind legs and put his front paws on the first bar of the stall. *That's better.*

Nell shifted her weight, brought her face down to his and nickered.

Dylan touched noses with her. *Are you sad because Mr. Tompkins gave you away?* His heart tripped. *Once I lived with Aiden in South Korea. I loved him and thought he loved me. When Aiden didn't want me anymore, he sent me to live with Casey. That made me sad.* Dylan's heart fluttered happily. *Now I have Casey and Casey has me. We'll always be together.*

Nell flicked her ears and looked away.

Dylan kept his paws on the bar and sidestepped until he was in front of her. *Now you have Tenn and Tenn has you. You'll always be together.*

Nell nudged Dylan with her head.

And you have me. Dylan gave her an openmouthed grin. *I've never had a horse friend before.*

"Dylan," Casey called. "Time to go."

It's going to be okay. Dylan slurped a kiss on Nell's nose. *Wait and see.* He dropped to all fours, ran halfway down the ramp, and jumped to the ground. *Hey!*

"What's the matter, Little Buddy?"

Dylan lifted a fluffy paw. *That.*

"Tenn," Casey picked up something in the grass, "you've got to see this."

Sumo came closer. "Is that a knife?"

"It's a multitool folding knife. I have one just like it." Tenn brought his own knife out and showed them. "All ranchers carry one. They come in handy."

"I have a knife." Casey took a Swiss Army knife from his cargo shorts pocket. "When we were in Oahu our friend Kekoa gave it to me. His grandfather was a Navy Seal and told Kekoa to always carry one."

"This one is really cool." Sumo pointed to the gadgets. "What is all that stuff?"

Casey opened up the knife and counted. "It's got fourteen different things. Pliers, scissors, two screwdrivers, a bottle opener and lots of stuff I don't know about."

"People use these multitools for fishing and camping, but ranchers use them every day. Last week I was riding in the hills, and I used this," Tenn showed them a tool, "to get a stone out of my horse's shoe. Another time I was riding and came across a bobcat. My horse spooked and ran through the trees. A branch got stuck between my horse and the cinch. I used the knife to cut the branch."

That's a handy knife. Dylan bumped Casey's leg. *What's a cinch?*

"A cinch is a strap that holds a saddle on a horse, Little Buddy."

Oh.

Sumo took the knife and turned it over. "Check this out."

"TR." Tenn ran a thumb over the etching and his mouth set in a grim line. "The Tompkins Ranch brand. Ronny must've dropped it."

Uh-oh.

Casey, Sumo, and Tenn exchanged looks.

"That means Ronny works for Mr. Tompkins," Casey said. "That means he was sent here to steal Nell."

Tenn nodded and slipped the knife into his jeans pocket.

That means Nell is in danger. Whine.

FIVE

Dylan's head bobbled on his shoulders, and he rocked from side to side as Tenn's truck bumped along the driveway. *My mouth won't stay closed.* The truck hit a pothole and Dylan's head snapped forward. *Ow!*

"We're here." Casey lowered his window to show Dylan the Tenn Hundred Acres Ranch sign. "Tenn Hundred Acres means Tenn's ranch is a thousand acres. He's like the biggest ranch owner in Lake Arrowhead."

I still don't get it. We're on land. We're not in a lake.

Sumo looked around him. "Why are these trucks here?"

"I hired Flynn Construction Company. They finished the new stable last week. It's big enough for twenty horses."

Casey's eyebrows shot up. "Do you have them already?"

Tenn's mouth turned up in a smile. "I'm working on it."

Sumo was into his cell phone and his fingers were dancing across the screen. "Whoa! Twenty horses is a boatload of money!" Sumo looked up. "Why get so many?"

"That's what it will take to do this right." Tenn gave a slight shake of his head. "When I was growing up in Brea, I dreamed of owning a ranch. Everyone thought I was crazy but here I am. I've never been happier."

Only you can make yourself happy.

Tenn pointed to a field marked by little flags and trenches. "Today they started digging the footings for the dining hall. Since the sports ranch will be for kids, I want everything casual and fun. I'm keeping the groups of kids small so instead of a lodge," he showed them a field to his left, "I built teepees. Each teepee will sleep four kids."

"That's so awesome, Dad."

"Most people will think I built teepees because I'm a Native American. Truth is," Tenn grinned, "I always wanted to sleep in one when I was a kid."

"Oh man, Little Buddy. Sleeping in a teepee would be so cool."

Dylan studied the white canvas wrapped around poles stuck into the ground. *Looks like an upside-down ice cream cone. Where are the beds?*

Sumo sat back in his seat. "You've done a lot."

"Thanks."

Casey leaned over Dylan to look out. "What's next?"

"Let's find out." Tenn lowered his window, cut the engine, and waved to two men looking at plans. "Jeff. Dave. How did it go with the inspector?"

One guy gave a thumbs up. "Wilcox was out an hour ago. We got the go ahead to pour the foundation."

"Great." Tenn nodded and started the truck. "I'll be down later."

Dylan watched trees and more trees whiz by. *I've never seen so many trees.* He leaned against the window, looked up and saw only a canopy of branches and long green needles. *The trees are very tall.*

"We're here," Tenn announced and turned off the engine. "Grab your gear."

Casey turned Dylan in his car seat and showed him a big house with a wraparound porch. "You'll like the porch swing. We can try it out later."

Okay!

Dylan waited for Casey to come around, unhook his harness and lift him out of the truck. When Casey put him down, Dylan wobbled. *Huh?* Dylan looked down at the chunky white rocks under his paws. *Feels funny.* He took two steps and the rocks made crunching sounds. *When Sumo has a soda, he chews the ice, and it makes crunching noises.* Dylan walked in a circle, liking the sound. *Fun!*

"The driveway goes around the house and to a huge garage. Tenn owns a bunch of cars, trucks, and tractors, so the garage has its own car wash."

Now he has a new truck. And a new horse trailer. And a new Harley. Dylan sighed. *I wish I had a Harley.* Dylan studied his paws. *I wish I could drive.*

Casey grabbed their backpacks, and they walked around the truck. "Tenn's house is as big as a hotel."

Pots overflowing with colorful flowers sat on the six front steps. Long fingers of reds, blues, and yellows shot from colored glass panes in the big wooden front door, leaving geometric patterns on the porch floor. *Pretty.*

"A stream is behind the pines," Casey crouched low and showed Dylan a group of trees, "and animals go there to drink." He turned Dylan and raised his muzzle up. "Our bedroom is on the second floor. The last time we were here a squirrel stayed outside the window."

Sumo joined them and slung his backpack over his shoulder. "Because you fed him."

"The squirrel was hungry. I had to feed him."

That's nice. You feed me when I'm hungry. Whine.

Sumo scowled. "Not at six o'clock in the morning."

"You started it. You fed the squirrel first."

Good Sumo.

"A little help guys," Tenn called from the back of the trailer.

"We just got here," Sumo complained, "and Dad is already putting us to work."

"Getting our bikes out is better than cleaning the tack equipment. Tenn has like a million saddles."

Dylan raced ahead and shifted from paw-to-paw while Tenn slowly lowered the trailer's ramp. *Hurry. I want to see Nell.*

Two kicks came from inside the trailer.

"Easy, girl." Tenn got Nell's attention by standing in front of her, but he stayed where he was. "We're home."

Nell answered with loud snorts and quick jerks of her tail. She kept her eyes on Tenn and laid her ears back.

"What's the matter," Casey asked.

Sumo tapped the screen on his cell phone and read, "Putting her ears back means she's feeling anxious."

It's like sign language.

"Now what?" Casey asked Tenn. "You can't leave her in there."

"And I can't force her out. She needs to come out on her own." Tenn put both hands on his hips and huffed out a breath. "This could take a while."

"What if," Casey dropped their backpacks on the ground and picked up Dylan, "Nell saw Dylan?"

"Try it."

Holding Dylan close, Casey walked slowly up the ramp. Nell cocked her head, stepped closer and gave a low whinny.

You're going to like it here. It's pretty.

Sumo had his cell phone up and video rolling. "Greetings Dylan's Dog Squad fans. We're at Tenn Hundred Acres Ranch in Lake Arrowhead. Meet Dylan's friend Nell."

Arf!

Casey angled Dylan so he was in the video with Nell. "Nell is a one-year-old quarter horse, and Tenn Hundred Acres is her new home."

Sumo posted the video. "Dylan's Dog Squad fans are going nuts over Dylan's road trip videos. Everyone wants to know if he'll ride a horse."

Me too.

"Absolutely." Tenn gave Dylan a wink. "Can't leave Dylan out."

Thanks Tenn.

Nell gave a happy snort and nuzzled Dylan's neck sending one fluffy ear flopping over his face.

Dylan shook out his ear. *I like you too.*

"She seems happier." Sumo put his cell phone in his pocket. "That's good."

"Nell likes Dylan." Tenn ran his hand slowly down her nose. He motioned Casey aside and reached for her halter. "Easy, girl," Tenn whispered. He slipped the halter over her head and clipped the lead rope on.

"Good job, Little Buddy." Casey hugged Dylan. "Now what?"

"After I get Nell down the ramp, I'm taking her to the old stable. Get your bikes out and take them to the hay barn. After that unpack your gear. I'll meet you for lunch."

"Lunch?" Sumo tried looking surprised. "Already? Maybe we should go to the kitchen and tell Mrs. Hudson we're here. You know," he finished lamely, "in case she's wondering."

And we can mooch something to eat. Dylan's stomach growled.

"Mrs. Hudson would like that." Tenn looked to the house. "She mentioned making potato salad for lunch. You can help her peel the potatoes."

Dylan studied his fluffy paws. *Not me.*

"We really, really want to. Honest, Dad," Sumo rounded his eyes and tried for serious, "but we brought a lot of stuff." He shook his head and switched to sad. "We should be responsible and put everything away first."

I have a backpack, Casey has a backpack, and you have a backpack. That's only three backpacks. I can count.

"Right." Tenn kept his grin to himself. "C'mon Nell."

Casey held up Dylan's paw. "Say goodbye to Nell."

Arf!

Nell went with Tenn but halfway down the ramp, she stopped and gave Dylan a long look over her shoulder. Tenn stroked her mane, leaving his hand on her shoulder. She snickered once before trotting along.

It's going to be okay. You're home now.

Balancing Dylan on his hip Casey wheeled his bike down the ramp and parked it off to the side. "Do you want down?"

Dylan kicked out both back paws. *Yes.*

Sumo rode his bike down the ramp and skidded to a stop next to theirs. He got off and did a three-sixty turn. "I wonder where the basketball court is?"

"If we ask Tenn to show us after lunch, he might forget about putting us to work."

"Good idea." Sumo dug his Angels cap out of his backpack. "Being on the ranch is great." He jammed the cap on his head. "Doing ranch work sucks. Getting up early, cleaning out the stalls and cleaning out water dishes takes forever. Then there's all that feeding and grooming. It really cuts into the day."

"Yeah, but we said we would help."

Sumo snorted. "You did. I didn't."

"Suck it up." Casey unzipped the screen on Dylan's bike trailer. "Hop in."

Do I have to? Dylan stretched himself forward on his front paws and then put it in reverse, sticking his rump up in the air. *Feels good to be standing.*

"You're right. I'm tired of sitting too. We'll walk the bikes over to the hay barn."

"Hold on." Sumo sent his backpack sailing onto the porch. Then he grabbed Casey's and

Dylan's backpacks and sent them flying.

"C'mon Little Buddy. The hay barn is up this hill and on the other side of the round pen."

Okay. Dylan trotted after Casey. *What's a round pen?*

"Walk slow," Casey warned. "Brea is three hundred and sixty feet above sea level. Lake Arrowhead is fifty-two hundred feet above sea level. The higher altitude makes it harder to breathe but you'll get used to it."

"Why does this ranch have so many hills?" Sumo clapped a hand to his chest. "I'm already feeling it."

Me too. Dylan panted along, letting his tongue hang out. *I changed my mind. I want to ride.* Dylan shook his topknot out of his eyes, picked up the pace and scratched at his bike trailer with one paw. *Hint, hint.*

Casey ignored Dylan and kept walking. "We're in the mountains. Duh."

Sumo got a better grip on the handlebars and trudged beside Casey. After a minute he said, "I get why Dad loves this place. It's really peaceful. Nothing ever happens here."

Casey stopped and faced him. "Not yet."

"Huh?"

"You're forgetting Tompkins sent Ronny to steal Nell. What's to stop Tompkins from sending another bad guy here?"

"Lake Arrowhead is ninety minutes from Brea." Sumo made a face. "It's over."

"Don't bet on it."

Listen to Casey.

"Why?"

"Maybe," Casey thought out loud, "Nell is more valuable than we know. Maybe that's why Tompkins went to all that trouble to send Ronny to San Bernardino. Tompkins wants to get her back, but Ronny messed up. He got arrested instead."

Serves him right. He kicked me. Twice. Dylan panted harder, his tongue dripping saliva on the ground. *Where's the hay barn?*

"That's a lot of maybes." Sumo wiped his sweaty forehead and turned his Angels cap around backwards.

Maybe not.

"Think about it," Casey persisted. "If Ronny blabs, they'll arrest Tompkins too."

"Not if," Sumo held up a hand, "Tompkins gets to Ronny first and shuts him up for good."

"How? The guy's in jail. Even if Tompkins did that doesn't solve the problem. Tompkins still wants Nell back."

That doesn't make sense.

"Why does he want her back so bad?" Sumo thought about that. "Sure, Dad thinks she'll be a great quarter horse —someday. That's a long time from today."

"We're missing something here," Casey muttered.

We're missing a lot.

"We need to talk to Dad."

Yes.

"Not yet. We don't know anything." Casey started pushing his bike again. "Besides, he doesn't seem worried."

"Hard to say with Dad. He's always calm. Nothing gets to him."

"Maybe we're wrong."

Don't think so. Talk to Tenn. Dylan felt the ground tremble under his paws. *Earthquake?* Dylan looked to Casey and Sumo, but they were talking and pushing their bikes along the path. *Uh guys?* Pounding sounds came out of nowhere and grew louder. Dylan searched the blue sky. *Thunderstorm?* Just then a hard gust of wind blew through the trees. *Ew!* He stepped back, wrinkled his nose, and then sniffed himself. *What smells?*

SIX

When Dylan rounded the bend, he put on the brakes. *I've never seen so many horses.* Brown ones, black ones, tan ones, red ones, their tails high and hoofs flying, all galloping in a big field. He scented the air. *Horse smells.* Dylan walked closer. Some horses idly cropped at the grass. Other horses hung their faces over the railing and watched him. Dylan wagged his little tail. *Arf!*

Dylan counted six horses fidgeting and stomping their hooves under the shade of the pine trees. *Six sweaty smelly horses.* Young guys with hoses splashed water on them and rubbed them down. One guy dipped a brush into a bucket of water and worked it over the horse's back and hips. The horse sent him a look, snickered, and kicked over the bucket. The guy sighed, patted the horse's chest, and righted the bucket.

I know how you feel. Dylan shook his head, sending his ears flapping around his face. *I hate getting wet all over.*

Dylan trotted past the horses and over to Casey and Sumo. They were leaning on a three-rail fence and watching an older woman lead a horse into the center of the ring. *The horse is by itself.* Dylan pawed Casey's leg. *Is it on time out?*

"Megan is the head trainer on the ranch." Casey picked Dylan up. "Want to watch?"

"The horses get exercised in the round pen every day." Sumo grabbed the top railing and climbed up, swinging both legs over to sit. "Each horse works with a trainer."

Oh. Like when Mom goes to the gym.

Megan stood next to the horse, holding a short rope with something on the end. She rotated the rope in a vertical circle. When the rope hit the ground the something on the end sent up little clouds of dirt. "Let's go Pax."

"Pax is a pinto," Sumo explained. "Pintos are brown horses with white splotches."

Mom says pintos are beans.

"Pax was a carriage ride horse in New York City. People think carriage rides are fun, but they're cruel. The horses work nine hours a day, seven days a week in awful weather and breathe in tailpipe exhaust. When they're too old to work, they're sold at auction." Sumo grimaced. "You don't want to know what happens to them. So, Dad rescued him and changed his name to Pax because it means peace. Dad wanted him to have a peaceful life."

That's nice. Dylan snuggled against Casey. *I like happy stories.*

"I heard New York City is trying to ban carriage rides."

Sumo nodded. "I hope it happens soon."

Dylan watched Pax toss his head. When Megan changed direction, Pax whinnied happily and kept going the other way. *Pax doesn't miss being a carriage ride horse. Wherever that is.*

"Pax," Megan called, "pay attention."

Pax snorted and pawed the ground but turned around.

Good boy.

"This exercise is called lunging," Casey explained. "It's good for the horses but they only do it for about twenty-five minutes. It can put stress on their joints."

"That," Sumo pointed to the rope Megan was using, "is a lunge line. It's also called a lunge whip but it's not really a whip. The little things on the end are lashes. They're soft and can't hurt Pax. The lashes signal Pax and control his speed."

That's good. What's a whip?

"Horses can run between twenty-five and thirty miles an hour," Sumo added. "Pretty amazing."

"How do you know this stuff?"

Sumo shrugged. "I read."

Casey hates to read.

"Trot," Megan said briskly.

Pax trotted. Megan stayed in the center of the round pen, turning slightly, and sending the lunge line in a high circle. The lashes lightly snapped the ground.

Walking in circles isn't much fun. When I go for walks, I get to smell everything. Dylan sighed. *Pax should go with me.*

After Pax circled the round pen twice Megan said in a higher, faster voice, "Canter."

What happened to Megan's voice? Dylan bumped Casey's chest. *She's talking funny.*

"Megan raises her voice and talks faster," Casey said, "to make Pax go faster."

She should just tell him.

"Canter," Megan repeated.

Pax tossed his head back. He added some speed, and his mane and tail flew behind him.

Now you're having fun. I like running too.

When Pax circled the round pen for the fourth time, Megan lowered and slowed her voice, "Slow down." Pax did. She let him go one more lap and then repeated in a deeper, slower voice, "Slow down." Pax shook his head and slowed to a walk. Megan went to him and reached for his halter. "Ho."

Pax bumped his cheek against her arm, rested his head on her shoulder and blew air through his nose.

"Okay, Pax." Megan laughed and got a treat out of her pocket. "You earned it." She held the treat out, palm up. Pax drew back his lips and nipped it cleanly from her hand.

Watching Pax work made me hungry. Dylan looked up at Casey and licked his lips. *Hint, hint.*

"Sorry. Your treat bag is in my backpack. I left it at the house, remember?" Casey rubbed Dylan's chest. "You're fine."

Am not. Whine.

Casey ignored him. "Now Megan will take Pax for a walk. After that she'll cool him down with water," Casey motioned to the group of horses under the trees, "so he doesn't get sick."

Getting sick is no fun. Getting a bath is worse.

"Casey! Sumo! I heard you were coming."

Sumo swiveled around on the railing. "We just got here."

Casey and Dylan turned around. "Harry!"

Dylan studied the little man in a plaid shirt and faded blue jeans. *He has a smooth face and pink cheeks. His head is round and shiny like the moon. He's not hairy.*

"I used to have hair like yours," Harry ran his fingers through Dylan's topknot, "but I lost it."

That's sad. Dylan waggled his head from side to side. *Where did you lose it?*

"This is Dylan. My brother Aiden sent him to me this summer."

"Howdy." Harry shook one of Dylan's paws. "You're one fine lookin' pup."

Arf!

"Boys," Harry waved a young guy closer, "meet Fernando Huertas. He got hired this morning and I'm showing him around. He's working his way West."

Dylan flicked his eyes to Casey. *We're in California. Even I know that's West and I'm a dog.*

"Where exactly," Casey asked.

Dylan leaned closer and sniffed Fernando. *Hmm.*

"Sorry." Casey pulled Dylan back and whispered, "That's rude."

I'm a dog. I sniff.

Fernando stepped away from Dylan. "New job. Next week. Horse ranch. Mexico."

You use little words. Dylan watched Fernando's lips move. *Where's May he co?*

Sumo frowned at Harry. "Does my dad know about this?"

"In a way." Harry took a bandana out of his back pocket and ran it over his smooth dome. "Tenn said to hire extra hands. We'll need help with the new horses he's getting for the sports ranch."

"But," Sumo pressed, "it seems weird to hire Fernando for a week."

"I work hard," Fernando interrupted. Angry fingers twisted the ragged cuffs of his leather gloves. "If I not wanted. Say so. I gone."

"Hold on, you two." Harry waved his bandana between them like a flag. "I checked Fernando's references myself and they're good. We're going to the old stable now to see Tenn. Want to come along?"

"We've got to put our bikes in the hay barn." Sumo hopped down from the fence. "After that we're going to see Mrs. Hudson."

Dylan ran a pink tongue around his muzzle. *And have lunch.*

"Okay." Harry gave Dylan a pat. "Have fun. C'mon Fernando."

Fernando shoved his gloves into his back pocket but didn't look back.

Arf! Dylan wiggled his butt. *Down.*

"When you're running around on the ranch," Sumo wiped his hands on his shorts, "watch where you're going. Horses aren't housetrained."

Huh?

Sumo pointed to dark clumps littering the ground.

It's dirt. So what? Dylan put his nose to the ground, sucked in air and backed up. *That's really stinky dirt.*

"It's horse poop, Little Buddy. If you step in horse poop it will stick to your paws. You'll smell like a horse, and Mrs. Hudson will make you get a bath."

Dylan's upper lip curled. *I'm not stepping in horse poop. I hate getting wet all over.* Dylan followed Casey, picking his way around the poop. *Horse trainers should carry poop bags. Dog owners do.* When they reached their bikes, Dylan scratched at his bike trailer. *Ride please.*

Sumo swung his leg over his bike and strapped his helmet on. "It's getting hot."

"Yeah." Casey unzipped the front screen and waited for Dylan to get in. "Race you to the hay barn."

"Okay." Sumo shoved off and pedaled hard.

Dylan pressed himself against the screen on his bike trailer. *Arf! He's going to beat us.*

"Relax." Casey took his time angling into his helmet. "When we get there, he'll be the one who is all hot and sweaty."

Sumo will be smelly, and Mrs. Hudson will make him take a bath. Dylan sank down on his comfy cushion and put his muzzle on his paws. *We won't smell.* He let out a happy sigh. *No bath for us.*

Dylan's bike trailer bounced along the road. After a few minutes he felt Casey slow the bike and stop. He leaned close to the side screen for a look. Long yellow and green stick things were flying by. More long yellow and green stick things covered the ground. *Very strange.* Dylan cocked his snout into the air and sniffed. *Something is very sweet.* He sniffed again. *A-a-choo!* His eyes closed and he hauled back his head. *Achoo! Achoo!*

"This is the hay barn." Casey helped Dylan out. "The old stable is big, and it has a hay loft. At feeding time, the hay gets tossed down and into the corral. The problem is the hay loft is too small to hold enough hay. So, the rest of the hay stays here until it's needed."

Achoo! Dylan's eyes watered. *It should be called the sneezy barn.* Dylan dropped down and rubbed a paw over his snout. *My nose is dripping.* He rolled onto his left side and then onto his right side, kicking out his paws and wiping his nose on the hay bits as he went. *Much better.*

"Hooray!" Sumo shouted and came over. "You lost!"

Dylan sat up and shook himself out. *Lost what?*

"We weren't trying to win," Casey teased.

Sumo used the hem of his T-shirt to wipe the sweat from his face. "Ha! You're just saying that."

No, we're not.

A big flatbed truck piled high with hay bales rumbled up the road and honked its horn. It made a U-turn and started slowly backing up toward the hay barn.

"Oh no," Sumo wailed. "The hay truck just got here. Now we'll have to wait."

Casey bent down and picked some hay out of Dylan's topknot. "It's pretty cool how they unload the hay bales. You gotta see this."

Can't! Loose hay was flying everywhere, and Dylan swiped at his eyes. *All I see is hay.*

The passenger door of the flatbed truck opened and a guy wearing a cowboy hat jumped to the ground. He hustled to the barn doors and opened them wide.

The truck is way bigger than Tenn's. Dylan started counting the truck's tires but when he got to ten, there were still some left. He sighed and gave up. *Too many.*

Cowboy Hat Guy went to the driver's side of the truck. "Ready." He pointed to the open barn doors with his right hand and his left hand made circling gestures in the air for the driver. "Easy does it Gilroy."

Dylan watched Gilroy straighten out the truck and then back it up until it was in front of the barn doors. *Uh-oh!* Dylan snuffled Casey's cheek. *The truck won't fit inside!*

"Don't worry. They've only hit the barn once. Bam!" Sumo clapped both hands together. "You should've seen it. Wood flying all over the place. Dad almost had a heart attack."

"No kidding. Tenn doesn't get worked up over anything."

"The truck took out the whole front of the barn." Sumo laughed. "But Dad wasn't mad about that. He was mad because he'd just painted the barn."

Ouch.

"Stop," Cowboy Hat Guy shouted and held his hand up. "Bring it down." A long ramp slid from the bed of the truck, stretched out and dropped to the ground.

"Let's get closer so Dylan can see."

Sumo brought out his cell phone. "Maybe they'll hit it today."

They walked to the side of the barn and waited. Gilroy poked his head out the window and said something to Cowboy Hat Guy.

Cowboy Hat Guy nodded. "Now."

Casey crouched next to Dylan and pointed. "See the thing under the hay bales? It's a conveyor belt and it moves the hay bales slowly to the end of the truck. If it goes too fast the hay bales will fall over and make a mess."

Dylan sat on his rump, leaned back, and counted seven rows of hay bales on the truck. *That's a lot of hay.* The big truck jerked once in place and a screech speared the air. *Yikes!* Dylan dropped to his belly and pawed his ears.

The conveyor belt began to roll. When the hay bales reached the ramp, they slid down and landed neatly on the ground.

"Oh, man." Sumo put his cell phone away. "I was hoping for some excitement."

You're weird.

Cowboy Hat Guy raised his hand and shouted, "Stop." Then he added, "Move forward."

The big truck rolled forward a few feet. More hay bales slid off and landed.

"Does Tenn really need all this hay?"

"You heard him. The new stable will hold twenty horses." Sumo brushed hay pieces from his face. "Dad's lucky to get this. Because of the drought in Northern California, there's not enough to go around."

Mrs. Hudson could make the horses something to eat.

"That stuff gets all over." Casey batted at the hay filling the air and knuckled his eyes. "Come here, Little Buddy."

Dylan got on his hind legs and put his front paws on Casey's thigh. *Good idea.* When Casey reached for him, Dylan hopped into his arms and buried his face into Casey's chest. *Phew! Hay makes a mess.*

"Too fast," Cowboy Hat Guy yelled. "Idle down."

When the last hay bale hit the ground and the ramp was brought up Cowboy Hat Guy ran around to the passenger's side and climbed in. The truck heaved forward and went down the road.

Casey, Dylan, and Sumo stared at the barn. Hay bales were stacked as high as the doorway and filled the inside.

Casey put Dylan down. "Can we get our bikes in?"

Uh, no.

"Dunno."

Nope.

Dylan trotted after Casey and Sumo. They turned sideways and squeezed past the hay bales. *It's dark in here.*

"Dad stores farm equipment and stuff over here." Sumo flipped the light switch on. Skis, mountain bikes, camping, and hiking equipment were against the wall, on hooks or on shelves. "We could move some of this over and bring in the bikes."

Not going to happen.

Casey went back to the barn door. "We'll never get the bikes past the hay bales. We could barely get inside."

"Oh, yeah."

There are a lot of smells in here. Dylan kept his nose to the ground and wandered over to the hiking equipment. Coolers were lined up according to size. Dylan bumped open one of the lids and stuck his face in. *No chow. Very disappointing*. He sniffed at a sleeping bag rolled up on a low shelf. *This is Tenn's*. He made his way past canteens, lanterns, first aid kits, camp stoves, and tool kits until he came to a big bag made out of thick material hanging on the wall. Dylan pawed at it, and it fell off the hook.

"Hey, Dylan found a really cool backpack."

It's a really big backpack.

"Dad does a lot of hiking and camping. That backpack holds everything."

"Exactly! Come here, Little Buddy." Casey laid the backpack on the ground and unzipped the top. "Get in."

Get serious.

"Look." Casey stuck his hand inside. "It's real roomy."

"Isn't it a little big?"

It's huge. I'm just a little guy.

"Nah." Casey held the backpack open for Dylan. "You'll be able to go horseback riding with us."

Since you put it that way. Dylan hopped in, turned around and looked up at Casey. *Now what?*

"We try it out." Casey tipped the backpack up on its end.

Yip! Dylan slid down inside and landed hard on his buns. *Ugh! It's dark in here! Really dark! Get me out!* Dylan punched out with front paws and kicked out with back paws. *Casey!* Dylan heard Sumo cracking up. *Not funny.*

"Hmm," Casey mumbled. "It's a little big."

You think?

"Come out, Little Buddy." Casey let the backpack drop to the ground.

Dylan fell forward face first. *Ow!*

Casey thought for a moment. "I could put a pillow inside for you to sit on."

My buns hurt. Dylan tummy crawled until he got to the

opening and poked his face out. *It'd better be a big comfy pillow.*

Sumo crouched low in front of the backpack and held his cell phone out. "Dylan's Dog Squad fans have to see this."

No, they don't. Dylan didn't budge.

Sumo took Dylan's picture, hit Send and put his cell phone in his pocket. "Now what?"

Casey sat back on his heels and looked around. "No way we're getting the bikes in here."

Told you. You never listen to me. Dylan's stomach growled. *I'm starving.*

"I vote for lunch. Let's get our bikes and go back to the house. We'll take the short cut."

Dylan jumped out of the backpack and headed for his bike trailer. *Race you to the house!*

SEVEN

Dylan charged up the front steps of Tenn's house and raised his paw to scratch at the front door.

"Wait!" Casey yelped and grabbed him by the shoulders. "We have to use the boot scraper first."

Dylan watched Sumo put one foot in something that looked like a big upside brush and drag his sneaker through. Dylan studied his front paws. *I'm not wearing boots.*

"Mrs. Hudson is nice," Sumo dragged his foot through again, "but she's a neat freak. If we bring dirt into the house...."

She'll make us take a bath.

"We won't eat," Casey finished for him. "She's even worse than Mom."

No way. Dylan got in line behind Sumo. *I want to eat.*

"Mrs. Hudson has five more rules." Sumo ticked them off on his fingers. "No banging doors, no shouting in the house, no running in the house, no running up and down the stairs and no dirty hands."

What about dirty paws?

"Other than that, she's awesome," Sumo said.

That's a lot of rules.

Casey nudged Dylan gently aside and ran his sneakers through the boot scraper twice. Then he stuffed his backpack into Tenn's backpack and wiggled both arms through the shoulder straps. He tossed Dylan's backpack to Sumo. "Take this."

"Okay."

"Here's the plan." Casey picked up Dylan. "We're going to sneak into the house and go to our room. We can't let Mrs. Hudson see us."

No. Dylan nuzzled Casey's chin. *Why?*

"I need to brush the gunk out of your fur."

Dylan looked at the hay stuck to his fur and the dirt clinging to his paws. *This is a lot.* He started to whine but stopped when Sumo put a finger to his lips, signing Quiet.

Sumo eased open the front door, poked his head in and whispered, "Let's go."

They started tiptoeing across the foyer and toward the stairs.

"Boys," Mrs. Hudson called.

"She's got ears like a rabbit," Sumo hissed.

"I heard that, Sterling Modragon."

"Uh, hi," Sumo warbled and bolted up the stairs. "Can't stop. We promised Dad we'd put our stuff away."

Casey hugged Dylan to him and took the stairs two at a time. "And wash our hands."

And brush my paws.

"Then we'll be down," Sumo added.

"Make it quick. Your dad is on his way."

"No problem," Sumo promised.

At the top of the stairs Casey and Sumo turned left and hustled down the hall.

"This is our room, Little Buddy." Casey bumped the

door open with his hip and put Dylan down. "Sumo's room is next door."

Sumo followed them in and tossed Dylan's backpack on the foot of the bed. "I'll be back."

"We'll hurry." Casey dropped to his knees, dug into Dylan's backpack, and rummaged around for his brush.

I like this room. It's pretty and gets lots of sun. The big bed looks comfy. Dylan sighed happily. *I like to stretch out when I sleep.* Dylan leaned against the bed and slowly rubbed his muzzle and right side along the white bedspread, leaving a long dirty streak as he went. *That felt great.* He turned and gave the bedspread his left side. Dylan shook himself out and thought about doing it again. *Uh-oh.* Twin trails of dirt stood out on the bedspread. *White gets dirty really fast.*

"Dylan," Casey's head was bent, and he was tossing things out of Dylan's backpack, "what are you doing?"

Nothing. Dylan double pawed the dirt on the bedspread, and it smeared. *I already did it.*

He jumped onto the bed, walked in a circle, and gave a little bounce. *Yup, comfy.* Dylan looked down and saw his dusty pawprints on the white bedspread. *Are my paws really that big?* He plopped down, then snuffled the pillow and it fell off. Dylan tummy crawled to the edge of the bed and looked down. *Oops.*

"Four Dylan's Dog Squad bandanas, really?" Casey put them on the floor.

I like to look good.

"You packed two alligator woobies." Casey complained and put the stuffed animals aside. "There's got to be like ten woobies in here."

I need all of them.

"Your brush has to be here somewhere," Casey muttered.

A breeze blew in and ruffled Dylan's ears. *Nice.* Dylan jumped down and trotted to a built-in wooden bench between two windows. He stood on his hind legs and sniffed along its long cushion, counting eight little pillows. *That's a lot of pillows.*

"Got it." Casey waved the brush and stood up. "Hop onto the window seat."

Okay. The pillows were in the way, so Dylan back kicked them to the floor. He sank to his stomach and gave Casey a canine grin. *Ready!*

"Dylan!"

What!

Casey pointed to the white bedspread covered in dirty pawprints and streaks. "If Mrs. Hudson sees that—and she will," Casey ran a hand through his hair, "she sees everything, we're dead."

So, I can skip the brushing?

Casey heaved out a breath. "We'll turn the bedspread down." He did that and frowned. "That won't work. Mrs. Hudson will check. She checks everything. She'll want to know why we turned the bedspread down. We'll tell Mrs. Hudson it's too warm for the bedspread. Yeah, that's what we'll say." Casey folded the bedspread into a square. "We'll hide it in the closet." He did, then faced Dylan. "Whew! That was close."

What came after we'll turn the bedspread down?

"Are you done?" Sumo came in and looked around. "Dylan looks the same. What are you doing in the closet?"

"Hiding the bedspread. Dylan got dirt on it."

Just a little.

"Are you serious?" Sumo's mouth dropped open. "Do you have a death wish?"

All this death talk is making me hungry. Dylan's stomach growled. *Hurry up and brush me. This may be my last meal.*

"You gotta help." Casey sat on the window seat next to Dylan. "Pick out the hay bits. I'll brush."

"Okay." Sumo squeezed in on the other side. "This stuff really sticks."

No joke.

Casey held onto Dylan's ear and tried to brush. The brush stopped.

Ow! Grr.

"Sorry, Little Buddy. It's stuck." Casey tried again. This time he began at the tip of Dylan's ear and slowly worked his way up.

Dylan flicked his ear. *Better.*

Sumo pulled hay bits out of Dylan's topknot and tossed them onto the floor. Then he got to work on Dylan's front paws. "At least you didn't step in horse poop."

I wouldn't.

Casey started on Dylan's other ear. "When is your mom coming home?"

"Don't know." Sumo flung a hay bit on the floor. "Why?"

"Just wondering how long we get to stay." Casey fluffed Dylan's ears out. "Not bad." He ran the brush down Dylan's back and tail.

Tickles. Dylan pushed out a back paw. *Don't forget.*

Casey pulled out hay and brushed. "I can't wait to take Dylan horseback riding."

"Boys!" Mrs. Hudson's voice came through the bedroom intercom. "Tenn is here. Lunch is in five minutes."

"We're almost done."

"Finished," she corrected.

Casey rolled his eyes. "She's just like Mom."

I hope she can cook like Mom.

Sumo gave Dylan the once over. "Not bad."

"Sit up straight." Casey gave Dylan's front legs and paws a quick brushing and then his back ones. "You'll do."

Arf! Dylan leaped off the window seat and charged down the hall. He took the corner wide, and his paws scrambled on the hardwood floors.

"Is someone running in the house?" Mrs. Hudson's voice came through the house intercom.

Yikes. Dylan skidded and did a bun burn at the top of the landing. *I forgot Rule Number Three.*

"Wait up, Little Buddy. We have to wash our hands."

I'll save you a seat. Dylan rolled his shoulders back, padded down the stairs and into the foyer. A long hallway went left and right. The doors to several rooms were open. *This is a big house.* Dylan went to the first room and walked inside. A couch and recliner chairs were arranged around a gigantic flat screen mounted on the wall. *That's bigger than the one we have at home.* Dylan heard Casey and Sumo clomping down the stairs, and he went back to the foyer.

"Uh," Casey sniffed his fingers. "What's this smell?"

"Soap." Sumo shoved his hands into his pockets. "Mrs. Hudson always buys the smelliest soap she can find. That's how she knows we washed our hands."

Mrs. Hudson is pretty smart.

"I hate it." Casey stuck his hands into his pockets.

Mrs. Hudson came into the foyer. When she saw them, a grin lit up her round face and she opened her plump arms wide. "Come here you two." She folded Casey and Sumo into a big hug. "It's been too long."

Casey broke away. "Meet Dylan."

Dylan trotted over. *Arf!*

"Oh my," Mrs. Hudson declared, putting both hands on her broad hips. "You're nothing but skin and bones."

Huh? Dylan looked himself over. *What about my fluffy fur? Whine.*

Sumo laughed. "Mrs. Hudson likes to feed people."

Excellent! Dylan slapped a paw on her knee and gave her a forty-two teeth grin. *I like to eat!*

"You're having lunch on the patio." She nodded toward the French doors. "Go ahead. Tenn is waiting. I'll bring the lemonade."

Dylan followed Casey and Sumo to the patio. *Something smells good.* He stretched up and sniffed. *Fried chicken, biscuits, strawberries, and potato salad. Yum.*

"Hi guys," Tenn said.

Dylan waited for Casey and Sumo to sit down and then wedged himself between their chairs. *This is the perfect spot. I can mooch from Casey.* He swung his head happily from Casey to Sumo. *Sumo's a slob. When he drops something, it's mine.*

"How's Nell," Sumo asked.

"Fine but I want to check on her in a few hours." Tenn reached for the potato salad. "I saw your bikes out front and put them in the garage."

"We couldn't fit them in the hay barn." Casey scooted his chair over to give Dylan more room. "So we brought them here."

"The hay delivery was more than what I expected." Tenn took some potato salad and passed it to Sumo. "The rest wasn't supposed to come until next week."

Casey picked up the basket of biscuits and put one on

his plate. "When we were at the hay barn, we figured out how to take Dylan riding with us."

"How?"

"We found your camping backpack. Dylan can ride in it," Sumo said. "It's a little big but we're going to put a pillow inside for Dylan to sit on."

A big comfy pillow.

Tenn raised his eyebrows. "Has he ever ridden in a backpack?"

Casey reached down and scratched Dylan's topknot. "Dylan rode in a harness when we went ziplining in Oʻahu."

Tenn gave a half laugh. "Close enough."

Arf!

Mrs. Hudson came out with a pitcher of lemonade and began to pour. "Casey pass the fried chicken."

Dylan stood on his hind legs, put his paws on the table and searched. *What about me?*

Casey nudged his paws off. "No paws on the table."

That's not one of Mrs. Hudson's rules. Dylan sat down and his shoulders slumped. *No chow for me.*

"Did Mom tell you," Casey put two pieces of chicken on his plate, "Dylan can't have chicken?"

"Ms. Donovan called this morning, and she said Dylan is allergic to chicken. I had no idea most dogs are."

"Mom researches everything."

Mrs. Hudson poured lemonade into Tenn's glass. "She also said Dylan is on a low-fat diet. After we talked, she emailed a list of what he can and can't have."

Mrs. Hudson is talking about me like I'm not here. Dylan tilted his head back and watched Casey pass the platter of chicken to Sumo. *I'm getting left out. Not fair.*

Dylan put his muzzle on Casey's thigh and licked his lips. *I'm going to starve. Whine.*

"Not to worry, Dylan," Mrs. Hudson said. "You're having roast beef and potato salad with a tiny bit of low-fat mayonnaise. I'll bring it right out."

That's it? Dylan whined. *I'm on a ranch. I want to eat what the guys eat.*

"Thanks Mrs. Hudson."

Sure, Casey. Take her side.

"Strawberries are the best." Sumo slid three onto his plate.

It's not nice to eat in front of me. Whine.

Sumo tried tossing a strawberry into his mouth and missed. It slid down his shirt and landed on the floor. He reached for another one.

Dylan pounced on the strawberry. *Yum.* He pawed Sumo's chair. *Drop another one.*

Mrs. Hudson came back with Dylan's dish, a placemat, and a bowl of water. She put everything down in front of him. "Here you go."

Yay! Dylan dove in and licked the bowl clean. *Seconds?*

"Thanks Mrs. Hudson."

"I'll be in the kitchen. Let me know if you need anything."

Casey, Sumo, and Tenn's heads were bent over their plates, but they nodded. Lunch had their complete attention.

When lunch had disappeared, Tenn pushed his plate away. "What do you want to do while you're here?"

"Can we ride around the ranch and see all the new stuff?" Sumo wiped his mouth with the back of his hand.

"We definitely want to go horseback riding so Dylan can try out the backpack. Right Little Buddy?"

Arf!

"Taking the boat out on the lake would be fun," Sumo added.

Tenn wasn't so sure. "Has Dylan ever been on a boat?"

"We did a Search and Rescue class on Catalina Island." Casey laughed. "He fell asleep as soon as he got on the boat and snored the whole trip."

Did not. Dylan flicked his ears and looked away. *Maybe just a little.*

"You're amazing Dylan. Someday I'd like to have a dog like you." Tenn sighed. "It's a big job to have a dog."

Casey and I are a team. We go everywhere together.

Casey slipped Dylan half a biscuit. "It's the best job I'll ever have."

Thanks, Casey.

"Don't forget." Sumo glanced at Casey. "We want to sleep in the teepee."

"Yeah."

Does it have a big comfy bed?

"All sounds good to me." Tenn got up. "Meet me in the garage in fifteen minutes. We'll take the Jeep."

EIGHT

Casey put Dylan in his car seat and dropped his backpack on the floor of the Jeep. "Lift up your muzzle." He slipped the seatbelt through Dylan's harness and clicked it into place. "Hold still." Casey ran his hand underneath it. "Not too tight."

Dylan waved his paw in the air. *Lower the window. Whine.*

Casey ruffled Dylan's topknot and went around to the passenger's side of the Jeep. When he got in, he smiled. "You're fine."

Am not. Dylan waited a beat and then licked his window. *Hint, hint.*

Casey rolled his eyes. "Tenn, could you lower Dylan's window?"

"Sure." Tenn pressed a button and Dylan's window went down.

Arf!

Sumo fastened his seatbelt. "Where are we going first?"

"The basketball court. Right now, it's just the court and bleachers. The scoreboard will go up next week." Tenn pulled the Jeep away from the house. "It's fun to get together with Harry and the horse trainers for a game. It's a great way to unwind at the end of the day."

Dylan hung his head out the Jeep window, letting his ears flap in the wind. *This is a great way to unwind any time.*

At the next turn, Tenn pulled the Jeep to the side of the road and pointed. "What do you think?"

It's like the basketball court at Carbon Canyon Park. Dylan looked beyond the court. *No concession stands. Bummer.*

"I put aside seven acres for the sports ranch. I want the teepees, the new stable, and the dining hall to be close together so the kids can walk to them."

Good idea. I like to be close to the chow too.

Tenn put the Jeep in gear. When the road curved, two deer bounded from the pines, gave them a wide-eyed look, and then froze in the middle of the road.

Dylan studied them. *You have big ears, little faces, big black noses, twitchy tails, and skinny legs. Kind of like horses.*

"Deer," Casey said to Dylan. "Like Rudolph the Red Nosed Reindeer."

Oh. Who is Rudolph?

A siren split the air and the deer leaped for safety.

"What's going on?" Sumo swiveled in his seat and looked around. "The siren sounded close."

"Over there." Casey pointed up ahead.

"The old stable." Tenn's mouth was grim. "We got trouble." He made a hard left at the next turn in the road and the Jeep's wheels spit up dirt and rock.

When they arrived a sheriff's car was already parked at the stable. Ranch hands stood by the stable door but stepped aside when the emergency vehicle rolled up. Two paramedics got out, opened the back, and pulled out a gurney. In an instant they were pushing it inside the stable.

Tenn got out of the Jeep and slammed its door. "Harry!"

Casey unbuckled Dylan's harness and lifted him out of his car seat. Sumo pushed his door open. They came around and stood by Tenn.

Harry broke away from the ranch hands and hustled over. "That was quick. I just texted you."

"Didn't get it. We were at the basketball court and heard the siren. What happened?"

"I checked on the horses and found Toby in Gypsy's stall. Geez, Tenn. Someone conked him on the head with a shovel." Harry's hand shook when he touched the back of his head. "He was out cold." Harry sucked in air. "I called 9-1-1 and then texted you. The deputies just got here."

"You did the right thing."

"I've never seen so much blood. It was everywhere." Harry squeezed his eyes shut. "We've never had trouble on the ranch before."

We got it now. Whine.

"The horses are riled up. I wanted to send the ranch hands in to calm them down, but the deputies said to wait." Harry scrunched his bandana into a ball. "What are we going to do? The deputies are calling the stable a crime scene."

Because it is.

"We need to let the deputies do their job." Tenn grabbed Harry by the shoulders and gave them a gentle shake. "I'm counting on you." Tenn looked toward the ranch hands. "Go over there and keep them calm. Don't let them start gossiping. We don't know anything yet."

Harry nodded. "Will do."

Tenn waited until Harry walked away. "I'm going to see what I can find out."

Casey, Dylan, and Sumo started after him.

Tenn turned around. "Where do you think you're going?"

"Tenn Hundred Acres Ranch is mine too. They," Sumo pointed to Casey and Dylan, "are my best friends."

"We're a team," Casey picked Dylan up.

We're Dylan's Dog Squad. We can help.

"Fine but don't get in the way. If the deputies tell you to leave, go back to the Jeep and wait for me. Got it?"

Casey, Dylan, and Sumo didn't agree. They just fell into step behind Tenn.

A tall deputy with a long face blocked the entrance to the stable. "Sorry, sir. You'll have to wait outside."

Tenn's voice was low and determined. "I'm Tennyson Stillwater. This ranch is mine and my man is in there. What can you tell me?"

"He's seriously hurt and hasn't regained consciousness. The paramedics are doing the best they can, and the hospital is standing by. He'll need surgery."

"Thanks." Tenn motioned to the stable. "Do you know who did this?"

"Deputy Gaines is in charge. He'll talk to you."

"Coming through," a paramedic announced.

They moved aside and Dylan looked down at Toby. He had a large white bandage wrapped around his head and a blanket was tucked around him. *Someone hurt you very bad.* Dylan watched the paramedic guide the gurney toward the emergency vehicle while the other paramedic held onto a clear plastic bag hanging from a silver pole.

"Mr. Stillwater?" A deputy came out of the stable and

handed Tenn his card. "I'm Deputy Gaines. What can you tell me about this man? Start with his name."

"Toby Renner has worked for me for about three years. He's quiet and does his job."

Deputy Gaines opened his iPad and got busy. "What's his job?"

"He's in charge of feeding and grooming the horses."

Deputy Gaines pinned his cop eyes on Tenn. "Any enemies?"

Tenn shook his head. "Everybody likes him."

Now Deputy Gaines shook his head. "Not everybody." He tapped the screen on the iPad. "What about you? Any enemies?"

Mr. Tompkins. Ronny the bad guy.

"My Dad's the best," Sumo blurted out. "Are you saying this is his fault?"

"Calm down." Tenn put a hand on Sumo's arm. "This is my son Sumo Modragon, his best friend Casey Donovan and Dylan. They're staying here for a few days."

"Hi." The deputy's tone was curt. "Let's get back to you. I noticed a lot of construction going on. Anybody upset about that?"

Casey hugged Dylan to him and stepped closer. "That's crazy. Tenn is building a sports ranch for kids. They'll learn to ride and play sports. Who wouldn't like that?"

Deputy Gaines said flatly, "You'd be surprised what upsets people."

"That can't be it." Tenn frowned. "I hired Flynn Construction Company to do the work. The owners have lived in Lake Arrowhead all their lives. Everything is going great. They just finished the new stable."

"Do you know everyone working for them? Everyone working here on the ranch?"

"No," Tenn admitted. "I've been gone a couple of days. My plan is to add twenty horses for the sports ranch, so my foreman Harry Biggs has done some hiring. He's a good man and always checks references."

Deputy Gaines stopped typing and looked up. "Where is Biggs now?"

Tenn pointed to where Harry was standing with the ranch hands. "He's the one in the plaid shirt, holding a bandana."

"I'll talk to him." Deputy Gaines made some notes before closing his screen. "When I know something, I'll get back to you."

"Thanks."

They watched Deputy Gaines walk away.

"Mr. Stillwater." Detective Melodia called and raised her hand in greeting.

Tenn returned the wave. "Detective Melodia. What brings you here?"

Detective Melodia was dressed in jeans, a cotton shirt, and boots. Behind her a boy was struggling to hold onto a leash. At the end of the leash a small dog with a smooth tan and black coat and black marble eyes was tugging and jumping wildly. In between tugs and jumps the dog shot out a little pink tongue.

She joined them and smiled. "Since we're meeting for the second time today, make it Liz."

"Call me Tenn. You already know Casey, Dylan, and Sumo."

"Noah had summer basketball practice at school today." Liz put a hand on Noah's shoulder. He looked up at her and watched her lips move.

That's how you read lips. Cool. Dylan moved his mouth around but gave up. *Oh yeah, I can't talk.*

"When I picked Noah up, I was telling him about your ranch. That's when I heard the 9-1-1 call come over the radio, and here we are." Liz signed to Noah and said, "Right?"

Noah signed back and said, "Right."

A series of quick huffs and puffs came from the end of the leash. This was followed by four tiny paws marching in the dirt.

Liz laughed. "Meet Billy da Pug. He and Noah are best buds."

"Hi," Tenn, Sumo and Casey said.

Arf! Casey and I are best buds. Dylan studied the little dog with the black mask face and curly tail. Dylan wagged his short, straight tail. *I wish I had a curly tail.*

Billy da Pug happily huffed out quick breaths. *Heh, heh, heh.*

Noah touched his mom's arm and then signed.

Liz turned to Tenn. "Noah wants to know if Billy da Pug can go off leash."

"Sure. Just watch him."

As soon as Noah released him, Billy da Pug bounced away on his stocky legs to an oleander bush.

"Fill me in," Liz prompted. "What have the deputies learned so far?"

"Nothing." Tenn scrubbed his hands over his face. "Toby is a good man. I can't believe anyone would hurt him."

"What if," Liz grew serious, "he's not the target. What if you are."

Dylan leaned against Casey's chest. *What if Liz is right.*

"No way," Casey began.

Tenn interrupted, "Everything is going great here. The building of the sports ranch is on schedule. I'm a lucky guy."

"Maybe your luck is running out," Liz said quietly.

Listen to Liz.

"Trouble seems to be following you today. First someone tries to steal your horse," Liz gestured to the emergency vehicle pulling away, "and now your guy gets hurt."

"You gotta find out who did this." Sumo clenched his fists. "My dad never hurt anyone."

"Since I'm here," Liz cocked her head toward the stable, "let's go in."

Tenn's eyebrows shot up. "We can do that?"

Liz grinned. "I'm a detective. Let me do all the talking." She got Noah's attention, signed, and said, "I'll be back. Stay here with Sumo and Casey."

Noah nodded.

"We're," Casey touched Noah's arm and then pointed to Sumo and Dylan, "learning American Sign Language, but we can't sign the way you do."

We only know words and commands.

Noah signed and said, "I read lips. I can talk but sometimes my voice sounds a little funny."

Not to me.

Billy da Pug let out a series of yips. He stuck his round butt in the air and got down on his front legs. He made soft growling sounds and then dove into the bush.

Dylan wiggled. *Down.*

Casey put Dylan on the ground. "Stay close."

Dylan wandered over to where Billy da Pug had his face stuck in the bush. *Your nose is smooshed in. How do you breathe?*

Billy da Pug backed buns first out of the bush. He swung his face around to Dylan and made happy heh, heh, heh sounds. Snot was dripping from his tiny black nose. His little pink tongue shot out and licked it clean.

Yeck. Dylan checked the bush out. *Not very interesting.* Dylan stretched up on his legs and searched the area. *Not much to see. Harry and Deputy Gaines are talking. The ranch hands are in front of the corral. The deputy is still in front of the door.* Dylan raised his muzzle high and felt the sun beat down on his topknot. *It's getting hot out here.* A squirrel made a mad dash from its tree to the shadows of the old stable. *A snooze in the shade would be nice.* Dylan trotted over to the old stable and Billy da Pug followed along.

No leaves. No vines. No nothing to curl up on. Dylan spotted a long wooden bench outside of the old stable. *It's in the shade but it doesn't look very comfortable.* Dylan jumped up, stretched himself out and laid his head down on the rough wood. *Nope. Too hard.*

Billy da Pug planted his front paws on the bench and tried an enthusiastic hippity hop with his back paws. His front half made it onto the bench. *Yip!* He slid back, whacked his chin and his plump rump plopped onto the ground. Billy da Pug got on his hind legs again. This time he brought his nose next to Dylan's and huffed out two short breaths.

Dylan sat up and shook his ears out. *This bench is too hard.* Dylan leaped over Billy da Pug's head. He landed and caught the sweet scent of hay. *Snoozing on hay would be better.*

Billy da Pug sidled up to Dylan, shifted from paw to paw and snorted.

Nell makes those nose sounds too. A loud whinny came from inside the old stable and Dylan's head whipped around. *That's Nell.*

Dylan saw the deputy on guard at the door click on his

radio and step away. *Casey said to stay close.* Dylan thought about that. *He didn't say not to go inside.*

Dylan looked over to Casey, Sumo, and Noah. Sumo had his cell phone out and was showing something to Noah. Noah laughed. Casey took the cell phone and scrolled through its screen. The three of them huddled over the screen and started laughing.

Dylan heard a louder whinny from Nell and made up his mind. *I'm coming!*

Billy da Pug fell in behind Dylan, and they scampered into the stable. When they got inside, Dylan slowed and scented the air. He turned right, passing stalls filled with horses. *Nell is this way.*

Nell was backed into the corner of her stall, head down and lightly pawing the ground.

Whine. Dylan stayed outside her stall. *It's okay. I'm here and I brought a friend.*

Nell fixed her dark brown eyes on Dylan. Her shoulders relaxed, she gave a slight shake of her head and slowly stepped to the gate.

Billy da Pug took that as an invitation and shimmied under her gate and into her stall.

No!

Nell reared up. Eyes flashed, ears went back, and her legs waved hoofs in the air. When she came down her hoofs struck the metal gate hard, and a loud sound rang out.

Voices came from the passageway and Dylan heard feet running. *Yikes!* He scooted away from Nell's stall, but he wasn't quick enough.

Tenn yelled, "Dylan!"

"Billy da Pug!" Liz shouted.

Paws don't fail me now! Dylan dug his paws in and took

off. Huffing and puffing noises told him Billy da Pug was right behind him.

Bright daylight lit up the entrance of the old stable and Dylan ran past the horse stalls. *I'm almost there.* Dylan tried picking up the pace, but he slipped on something, and his paws flew out from under him.

"Dylan, stop!" Tenn insisted.

Dylan did a side slide, sending up dirt and hay. He struggled to his paws and started to take off but then he saw what he'd slipped on. *It's a glove.*

NINE

"Dylan," Tenn shouted, "get back here."

No way.

"You too Billy da Pug," Liz called.

Dylan heard Tenn and Liz coming and ran faster. When he reached Casey, he got on his hind legs and pawed punched Casey's thigh. *Arf!*

"Hey, Little Buddy." Casey started to crouch down.

Dylan saved him the trouble and leaped into his arms. *Help me.*

"You're shaking." Casey brushed Dylan's topknot out of his eyes. "What's this?" Casey gently tugged the glove free from Dylan's jaws.

Look familiar? Fernando had gloves like this.

Tenn jogged up to them and held both hands out to his sides, palms up. "What happened to you watching Dylan and Billy da Pug?"

Sumo, Casey, and Noah exchanged looks.

Dylan squirmed and kicked out with his back paws. *I should go now.*

"Stop wiggling," Casey insisted, struggling to hold on.

"You're going to fall." Dylan wiggled harder so Casey shoved the glove into his cargo shorts pocket and used both hands to hold onto him. "We were watching," Casey began, "but not all the time."

"What's the big deal?" Noah asked and signed.

"Dylan and Billy da Pug were in the stable. The stable is a crime scene." Liz tapped Noah's arm. "You know better."

Noah narrowed his eyes. "Whatever."

Liz gave him The Look and quickly signed something.

Wow! Liz can sign fast.

Noah made a face.

Dylan watched Noah sign something back, really fast. *I wish I could sign like that.* Dylan looked at his fluffy paws. *I wish I had fingers.*

"The deputies are trying to find out who hurt Toby." Tenn kept his voice even. "Dylan and Billy da Pug could've destroyed valuable evidence."

"Like what?" Sumo argued. "Where were Dylan and Billy da Pug?"

Tenn gritted his teeth. "They were in Nell's stall."

"But," Noah said and signed, "you and the deputies were in Gypsy's stall. That's where Toby got hurt."

"Relax," Casey chimed in and gave Liz and Tenn his best smile. "Since Dylan and Billy da Pug were in Nell's stall there's no way they could've messed up anything."

I found Fernando's glove in the old stable.

"You're right." Tenn gave Dylan's shoulder a pat. "I'm sorry I yelled at you."

Dylan bumped Casey's chest. *Show them the glove.*

"It's okay." Casey gave Dylan a hug. "Tenn's not mad at you."

Dylan sighed and gave up. *You never listen to me.*

Loud heh, heh, heh sounds erupted, and everyone looked down to see Billy da Pug panting and dancing around Liz's legs.

You don't like to be left out.

Liz laughed and reached down to give him a pat. "I'm sorry I yelled at you too."

"What happens now?" Casey shifted Dylan to his other side. "Will they keep looking?"

"Detective Melodia," the deputy guarding the door called. "Deputy Gaines wants you to stay and help. We're shorthanded."

"I knew it," Liz said under her breath, but she sent him a wave. "Be right there." Liz faced Noah and gave him a thin smile. "Bad news," she said and signed. "They're shorthanded. They want me to help for a while."

"No!" Noah kicked the dirt with the toe of his sneaker. "You promised we'd watch the zombie movie marathon tonight."

Movie marathons are the best! Dylan sat up straighter and nuzzled Casey's cheek. *We can watch movies and eat junk food. What is a zombie?*

"I wish we could. I'll call Gram and ask her to come over. You'll like that."

"No, I won't. Gram knows zip about zombies," Noah crossed his arms over his chest, "and she always wants to sit with me." He glared up at her. "What am I, five?"

"Gram means well."

Noah turned his back on her.

That's funny. Dylan gave Noah a canine grin. *Now your mom can't talk to you.*

Tenn broke in. "We like zombies. Right, guys?"

"Oh yeah," they chorused.

"Zombies are so cool, Little Buddy. They're like six feet

tall and skinny with long stringy hair." Casey bared his teeth. "They got pointy fangs, and they eat people."

Yikes. Do they eat little dogs?

"Liz, go to work." Tenn stepped in front of Noah. "You and Billy da Pug can come to my house. We'll hang out and barbecue before the marathon."

And eat junk food.

Noah's sneaker was kicking the dirt again. "Do you have a flat screen TV?"

"The biggest."

Noah's eyes lit up. "Can I Mom?"

"It would really help me out," Liz hesitated, "but I don't know how long I'll be."

Sumo grinned at Noah. "Awesome."

Liz wasn't so sure. "We just met you today. I don't want to be a bother."

"Aw Mom. Now you sound like Gram."

"We got this covered," Tenn promised. "If you're going to be late, text me. Noah and Billy da Pug can stay over."

Casey, Noah, and Sumo high-fived each other. "Sleepover!"

"Well," Liz wavered. "Do you have your cell phone?"

Noah patted his shorts pocket.

"Okay." Liz gave Noah a quick hug. "Be good."

"Yeah, yeah."

Liz quickly touched the fingertips of her right hand to her lips and then moved her fingers down and toward them, signing Thank You. "Bye!" she added and took off.

"What now," Sumo asked.

"I'm calling Mrs. Hudson," Tenn pulled his cell phone out of his pocket, "and telling her we've got company for dinner. Then we'll go to Lake Arrowhead Market and pick up some manly men grub for dinner."

"I want Cheetos," Sumo said.

I like Cheetos.

"Can we get watermelon?" Casey grinned. "It's a fruit so it's good for you."

I really like watermelon.

Tenn waited for Noah to look at him. "What sounds good?"

"Well," Noah dropped his eyes to his sneakers.

"You're our guest," Tenn prompted. "You get to pick. What do you want for dinner?"

"Steak!"

I love steak. Dylan licked Casey's cheek. *Things are looking up.*

Tenn called Mrs. Hudson and filled her in. He ended with, "We're barbecuing tonight. Need anything at the store?" He listened for a bit and then interrupted. "It would be better if you call it in. We got some things to do first. Tell Hank I'll pick everything up this afternoon." He listened again. "No news about Toby. Deputy Gaines said he would call me later."

"How did Mrs. Hudson find out so fast," Casey whispered to Sumo.

"She's got a police scanner in the kitchen. She listens to it like some people listen to music."

"Uh-huh. Uh-huh. Yeah. Thanks." Tenn shoved his cell phone into his pocket. "Okay, boys. Pile into the Jeep."

Sumo raced around to the front of the Jeep. Casey put Dylan into his car seat before getting into the back seat. Then he scooted over so Noah could climb in with Billy da Pug.

This is a tight fit. Whine.

Tenn turned around so Noah could read his lips. "I can go by the house, and we could take the truck."

"Nah." Noah put his seatbelt around him and Billy da Pug. "We're fine."

They bounced along the ranch road. When Tenn reached Highway 189, he turned left.

"Lake Arrowhead Market is the other way," Noah said.

Tenn raised his chin up and spoke into the rearview mirror for Noah. "It is but Lake Arrowhead and my boat are this way."

Cheers went up all around.

Arf!

"Sumo showed me pictures of Tenn's new boat." Casey brushed Dylan's topknot out of his eyes. "It's super cool."

Noah leaned forward and tapped Tenn on his shoulder. "Can we drive the boat?"

People drive cars not boats. Don't get it.

"Yeah *Dad*." Sumo turned halfway in his seat so Noah could read his lips. "We have to. We're only here for a few days. Who knows when we'll be back. Besides, *Dad*," Sumo slid a look to the back seat, "Noah is our guest. You always say guests get to pick what they want."

Tenn lifted his face to the rearview mirror again and caught Noah's eye. "We'll see."

"Yes!" Sumo leaned over his seat and high-fived Casey and Noah.

Casey hugged Dylan. "We'll see always means yes with Tenn."

Arf!

"Don't tell Mom, okay? It'll be a secret."

Sure. Dylan turned his big brown eyes up to Casey's. *If I get to drive the boat too.*

Lake Arrowhead Village was packed with sunshine, mile high blue sky, fat white clouds, tourists and people walking their dogs. Instead of heading into the parking lot

Tenn found a parking space in front of the real estate office and got out. "The Bluegrass Music Festival started today so the main parking lot will be packed."

Dylan waited while Casey clipped his leash to his collar. *Lake Arrowhead Village is full of smells. Water. Pine trees. Yummy food.* A brown and yellow bird dipped its wings and skimmed over Dylan's head. *Arf!* Dylan jumped back. *I wish I could fly.*

They cut across the parking lot and took the ramp by the sandwich shop. Jewelry shops, art galleries and clothing stores were doing a booming business. They had to walk around a crowd waiting to get into a corner restaurant with an outdoor patio.

Dylan tugged on his leash. *Something smells good.*

"That's Belgian Waffle Works, Little Buddy. When we visit Tenn in the winter, we'll go there. They have the best waffles and the best hot chocolate."

Big wow. Dylan's step slowed. *I can't have chocolate.* Then he perked up. *I can have waffles!*

"The boat is this way." Tenn led them past the Lake Arrowhead Queen Tour Boat where men, women, kids, and dogs were lined up at the dock. Most people were wearing hats, and everyone smelled liked coconut sunscreen. "Great day for a tour of the lake."

"I remember when we took the tour." Sumo dug his baseball cap out of his backpack and stuck it on his head. "It was good but you're better."

"Glad to hear it."

Sumo turned around and started walking backward. He pulled his cell phone out of his pocket and held it up. "Smile everybody." He pressed video. "Greetings Dylan's Dog Squad fans. We're taking my dad's new boat out on

Lake Arrowhead, a seven-hundred-and-eighty-acre, man-made lake."

Noah cut in. "How do you know this? I don't know this, and I live here."

Casey bumped Noah's arm and faced him. "Sumo reads."

Noah made a face. "Why?"

"Beats me."

Tenn stopped in front of a sleek white boat with gleaming brown leather interior and a white hardtop. "Casey, Dylan and Noah meet Scout."

It's the prettiest boat here.

"Well, if it isn't Tenn Stillwater, Lake Arrowhead's hotshot rancher," a gravelly voice snarled from the ancient boat tied up next to Tenn's.

"That's Jed." Tenn motioned for them to get on board. Casey, Sumo, and Noah stayed where they were.

A tall man stepped out from under a faded and torn blue canvas boat top and glared at them. "You got some nerve tearing up our ancestor's land to build your fancy sports ranch." His bronze face was hard and lined. A streak of white shot through jet black hair that hung in a thick braid down his back. "You're destroying years of Native American heritage."

"Watch your tone." Tenn gestured to Sumo, Casey, and Noah. "Kids are here."

The man's mouth twisted up. "Just like you to hide behind a bunch of no neck monster kids."

And dogs. Grr.

"You got a problem with me, Jed? Take it to Sheriff Ridley."

"Good idea." Sumo got busy with his cell phone. "This guy's a weirdo."

Noah shook his head. "He's weird but he's not dangerous. My mom says he calls the station at least once a week complaining about something."

"What's his problem," Casey said a little too loudly.

Tenn kept his voice low. "When I applied for permits to build the sports ranch, Jedidiah Nightwalker was the only one on the mountain who voted against it. He had a ranch up here, but he had some hard luck and lost it. Now he spends his time on his boat."

Dylan studied the sad little boat bobbing on the water. *The paint is peeling off. The motor is covered in rust. It looks like it could sink any minute.*

"Just what we need up here," Jed's mouth turned down and he fisted his hands on his hips, "more tourists. All they do is clog up the mountain road with their expensive cars and leave their trash all over the place. Then there are the city slickers who come here and buy up all the good land. The next thing we know we got another hotel or restaurant." He shook his head in disgust. "They got no business sense, and the business goes bust. We're left with abandoned buildings until the next nitwit comes along."

Sumo stepped up. "My dad's not doing any of those things!"

Tenn grabbed Sumo by his arm. "Let it go."

"Sumo's right," Casey insisted. "Tell him to mind his own business."

Yeah!

"Your land was home to the Paiute and Serrano nomadic tribes. You," Jed jabbed an index finger in the air between them, "are destroying Native American sacred burial sites for some lousy sports ranch."

"A study was done, and no burial sites were found,"

Tenn assured him. "If something is discovered I'll stop the project. You have my word."

"Ha!" The angry index finger was back. "You're just saying that to look good in front of the kids."

Tenn ignored him. "Get on the boat, boys. The day is too good to waste."

"We're not done here," Jed shouted. "You're going to pay."

TEN

Sumo got onboard first and then helped Noah and Billy da Pug get on. "Dad says everyone has to wear a life jacket on the boat."

"What about Billy da Pug and Dylan?" Noah scratched the panting pug's head. "They're too small for one."

"No life jacket, no getting on the boat."

"Oh yeah." Casey and Dylan stopped where they were. "Dylan has a dog life jacket for surfing, but I didn't bring it. Does that mean he can't go?"

Don't leave me. Dylan's ears drooped. *I want to go too.*

"No problem." Tenn motioned them on. "Sometimes friends come onboard with kids and babies. I have life jackets with," Tenn wrapped his right hand around his left arm, "those floatie things." He lifted a bench seat and gave a tiny jacket to Noah. "Try this on Billy da Pug." He pulled out a bigger one and tossed it to Casey. "This should fit Dylan."

Casey caught it one-handed. "Thanks."

Arf!

Tenn lifted the lid on another bench seat, took out three

life jackets and dropped them on the deck. "Try these on." He brought one out for himself and shrugged into it. "We'll take off as soon as you're ready."

Casey helped Dylan into his life jacket and adjusted the straps. "You look pretty sharp."

Dylan looked down at the bulky lime green life jacket. *I look pretty fat.*

"Stay still Billy da Pug!"

Dylan peeked around Casey. Noah had gotten Billy da Pug into the life jacket, and now the pup was having a grand time rolling around on the bench.

"Okay everybody." Sumo dug his cell phone out of his shorts pocket. "Group video."

Billy da Pug launched himself into another body roll. Noah made a grab for him but missed. Billy da Pug rolled too close to the edge and did a spectacular backflip on the way down. *Yip!*

Sumo's cell phone caught the whole thing on video including the pup's landing. His sturdy legs were splayed out on the deck in four different directions.

"Oh man." Sumo was laughing so hard he dropped his cell phone. "Billy da Pug looks like a capital H."

That's gotta hurt. Whine.

Billy da Pug blinked and wobbled to his paws. Then he plunked his plump rump on the ground, looked up at everyone and let his little pink tongue hang out.

"He does stuff like that all the time." Noah picked up the little dog and put him on the bench. "He's okay."

You're one funny dog. Dylan sent him a big canine grin. *I like you.*

The boat's engine came to life and Tenn eased the boat away from the dock. Out in the water he opened up the throttle.

"I bet this baby can really move." Sumo knelt on the boat cushion and leaned over the railing, watching the dark blue water churn up. "I can see the bed rocks."

"The water is really low because of the drought. The buoys are marking two hundred feet from shore as the five miles per hour zone." Tenn tossed Sumo a glance. "Sit down while the boat is moving."

"The drought sucks." Sumo turned around and plopped down onto the bench. "Did you know Lake Arrowhead was originally Little Bear Lake? A bunch of rich guys bought it in 1920 and changed the name. They said the San Bernardino Mountains looked like an arrowhead."

Noah sent Casey a look, put his index finger to his chin and twisted it, signing Seriously.

Casey made his hand into a fist and bobbed it back and forth, signing Yes. Then he rolled his eyes.

Dylan sighed. *Sumo's been reading again.*

"Anyway," Sumo continued, "they wanted rich people to come here so between 1921 and 1923 they spent eight million bucks, built a bunch of expensive buildings, and called it Lake Arrowhead Village. For a while movie stars came but by the 1970s everything was falling apart. It got so bad the fire department began a "Burn to Learn" program and used the buildings to practice on."

That's sad.

Sumo leaned back against the boat cushion. "Later more rich guys came along and pumped more money into the Village. They built new buildings and Lake Arrowhead Village reopened in 1981."

That's nice. I like it here.

"Are you always like this," Noah asked Sumo.

"Yes!" Casey laughed.

Yes!

Sumo's face went blank. "Like what?"

Tenn slowed and then cut the engine. "This is a good spot."

Dylan liked it when the boat started rocking gently side-to-side. *The sun is toasty.* He lifted his muzzle high, and the lake breeze blew his ears away from his face. *I'm getting sleepy. Time for a world class snooze.* Dylan relaxed and let his front legs slide out in front of him. Something had him stopping halfway. *What?* He checked himself out. *This life jacket is like wearing a big lime green pillow.* Dylan dug his front paws in and pushed back on the smooth leather seat. The boat tipped on the water, and he lost his balance. *Agh!*

"Dylan!" Casey caught him.

"Whoa!" Sumo cracked up. His cell phone was out, and video was rolling. "You almost did a Billy da Pug backflip. Wait until Dylan's Dog Squad fans see this."

Not funny. Grr. Dylan leaned against Casey and licked his cheek. *Thanks for catching me.*

"You need to be really careful on the boat, Little Buddy."

Dylan slapped a paw on Casey's knee. *You really need to give me a treat. Whine.*

Casey got the hint and took the treat bag out of his backpack. "Mom packed oatmeal cookies."

Across from them Billy da Pug's little paws shuffled from side-to-side on the boat cushion. *Heh, heh, heh.* His shiny eyes were glued to the treat bag.

Casey showed Noah the treat bag. "Can Billy da Pug have a treat?"

"Only a little. Pugs are good little eaters." Noah pulled Billy da Pug close to him. "Mom makes a big deal about what he eats."

"My mom does too." Casey broke a cookie in half,

passed it to Noah and gave Dylan the other half. "Drives me nuts."

"Ms. D is cool," Sumo insisted. "At least she cares."

"Your mom cares," Casey said.

Sumo shrugged. "I guess."

Sumo wishes he had a mom like ours. Dylan gulped down the cookie and panted in Casey's face. *Thirsty.*

"Mom's okay." Casey rummaged around in his backpack for Dylan's collapsible water dish and filled it to the brim. "Here you go."

Dylan lapped the dish dry, raised his head and let his muzzle drip onto Casey's shorts. *Thanks.*

Casey showed Dylan's dish to Noah. "Can Billy da Pug have some water?"

"Sure."

Billy da Pug sniffed the water, licked his lips, but ignored it. He raised his face up to Noah's. *Heh, heh, heh.*

"Uh-uh." Noah shook his head.

Billy da Pug disagreed, let out a low whine, and planted his front paws on Noah's leg.

Noah tapped his two fingers to his thumb, signing No.

Billy da Pug jumped down, went over to Casey and locked marble eyes onto his.

"Don't give him anymore." Noah scooped Billy da Pug up and put him on the bench. "He's had enough."

Dylan rubbed his muzzle across Casey's lap and gave him the big brown eyed stare. *C'mon. One more.*

"Sorry." Casey put the treat bag in his backpack, then showed Dylan his empty hands. "No more."

Tenn nodded to Casey. "You're up first."

"Great." Casey picked Dylan up. "You'll like this."

Dylan studied the boat's wheel. *It's like the steering wheel in our car.*

"Nothing to it." Casey put him on the seat. "It's like driving a car."

Mom uses two hands when she drives. Dylan flapped his front paws between him and the wheel. *I can't drive.*

"You're too far away." Casey frowned. "Lean closer. Look straight ahead. Don't look down. Don't look at the wheel."

That's a lot of rules.

"Try it."

I can't lean closer. I can't see straight ahead. I can't see over the wheel, and I can't reach the wheel. Whine.

"Dylan can't drive the boat, Casey."

Hey! Dylan whipped his head around to Tenn. *Don't be so negative.*

"I'll hold him for you."

I want to drive the boat too. Dylan dodged Tenn when he reached for him. *Grr.*

"Wait a second." Casey picked Dylan up and slipped onto the seat with him. "No wiggling or you'll fall off."

Not me. Dylan couldn't help it and wiggled his buns.

"This is the instrument panel." Casey pointed to round glass things on a wooden thing in front of them. "They tell you important stuff." He touched one. "Like how much fuel is left."

Good to know.

"Can Dylan swim?"

Dogpaddle.

"Sure. We surf, go to swim parties and to the beach all the time. Why?"

"It's getting crowded out here." Tenn pointed to the red and white boat speeding past them. People were sitting on the boat's railings and running on the deck. A fast game of frisbee was underway. A guy went after it, missed, and slammed into the railing as the frisbee sailed into the lake. "No one is wearing a life jacket." He glanced back to Lake Arrowhead Village. "It's a long swim to shore."

We're way out in the middle of a huge lake. Dylan craned his neck to shore. *I can barely see the shops.* Dylan nuzzled his life jacket. *Forget about swimming to shore. I'll just kick back and float.*

"How long can we stay out?"

"Not long. After Noah and Sumo take a turn at the wheel," Tenn said, "we'll head back to the dock. Let's go."

Yes! Dylan studied the wheel. *Now what?*

Casey started the boat. "To turn the boat," Casey leaned forward and placed Dylan's paws on the wheel, "do this," Casey held them in place, "slowly."

Dylan felt the boat turn and his heart skipped happily. *This is fun.* He gave Casey a tongue-hanging-out-of-his-mouth grin. *I like this!*

"Now straighten the wheel out." Casey helped him.

I'm driving the boat! Dylan's eyes dropped to his paws on the wheel and the boat tipped.

"Don't look at the wheel. It's doing fine. Always look where you're going."

Noah and Billy da Pug came over to watch. "How do you know this stuff?"

"Tenn taught us when we started coming up here." Casey put Dylan's paws on the wheel again. "In case of an emergency he wanted us to know what to do."

Noah came closer. "This is so awesome."

Tenn waited for Noah to look at him so he could read his lips. "Boat safety is number one. Since we're on the lake a lot, it makes sense to know it."

"Yeah, but the boat is the really cool part. Especially

when we go fast." Casey caught himself. "Oh hey. If you ever meet my mom, don't tell her about this."

"Why?"

"There's some dumb law that says kids have to be eighteen to drive a boat with a captain."

"A captain," Noah echoed.

"That's Tenn." Casey grinned. "If we didn't have Tenn, we'd have to be twenty-five."

"Uh. I'm only eleven."

"Yeah, but together, you, me and Sumo are thirty-five."

Don't forget me. Dylan cocked his head. *I'm nearly two.*

"My mom's a detective, remember? If the lake patrol stops us when we're driving the boat, I'm busted. I'll be on restriction for the rest of my life."

Oh yeah. Us too.

"Today you're only learning the basics and I'm right here." Tenn took Billy da Pug from him. "Want to try it?"

Noah's face lit up. "Oh yeah."

Casey helped Dylan off his lap and held onto the wheel until Noah sat down.

Dylan tuned Tenn out when he started going on about boat safety. *Boring.* Dylan wandered to the back of the boat and sniffed around a bit. *Nothing interesting.* He hopped onto the bench next to Sumo and spread out. When the boat picked up speed Dylan sighed. *I learned to drive a boat and the sun is out. It's a great day.*

"If we had skis," Sumo tossed his Angels cap onto the boat bench, "we could go jet skiing."

Sure. Dylan squinted at Sumo in the bright sunlight. *What's jet skiing?*

"I wonder if the water is cold." Sumo knelt on the bench, put his elbows on the railing, and studied the water. "Jet skiing sucks big time if the water is cold." He bent over the railing trying to catch a spray of water. "Not close enough." He started to lean out farther but stopped and sneaked a look at his dad.

Tenn told you to sit down.

"Dad always freaks out about this safety stuff." Sumo moved Dylan over and laid down on the bench. He shoved one arm through the railing, but he still couldn't reach the water. "The water is probably too cold."

That's too bad.

"Hmm." Sumo was back on his knees and leaning over the railing again. "Only one way to find out."

Don't do it. Whine.

Sumo put a finger to his lips, signing Quiet. He grabbed the railing with both hands and hitched himself up and halfway over. "Nothing to it."

Two speed boats zipped past, racing each other, and sending up waves of water. Tenn's boat rocked and heaved to the side.

Ugh! Dylan gripped the bench with both paws and looked to the front of the boat. *This is scary.*

"Hey!" Tenn cupped his hands to his mouth and yelled, "Slow down."

"Help!" The wheel slipped out of Noah's hands and the boat pitched. "What do I do?"

Tenn shifted Billy da Pug to his hip, reached around Noah and grabbed the wheel with one hand. "Hold it steady." The boat heaved again, and Noah struggled to keep it even. "You can do this."

Dylan hung onto the bench. His body rocked back and forth like a metronome.

"What's going on?" Sumo straddled the railing and tried for a better look at the front of the boat.

Sit down Sumo.

The boat rolled.

"Holy, moly, joly!" Sumo shrieked and fell over the railing, both arms windmilling wildly.

Arf! Dylan pulled himself into a sitting position. *Guys! We need help! Arf!*

Casey called back without looking. "It's okay."

Nuh-uh! Sumo is in the lake! Dylan poked his face through the railing and searched the water.

In a heartbeat Sumo bobbed to the surface. He waved his cell phone over his head. "Dylan! You gotta save my cell phone!"

Arf! Dylan looked from Sumo to the front of the boat and shifted from paw to paw. *I gotta get help. Arf! Arf!*

"Quit barking and come get my phone. It'll get ruined in the water. You can hold it in your mouth."

If your phone is in my mouth, I can't bark. Then no one can save you.

A wave slapped Sumo in the face. "The water is freezing!"

I don't like freezing water. I'll get Casey!

With every wave Sumo's life jacket rose up and hit him in the face. "This life jacket is stupid." Sumo was struggling to hold his cell phone high in the air with one hand and his other hand was treading water like crazy. His teeth were chattering like a monkey's. "Hur-ry!"

Arf! Arf!

A third boat ripped past followed by a fourth, drenching Sumo in their wake and making Tenn's boat rock violently.

Dylan stumbled across the deck and over to Casey. *Help!*

"Don't worry." Casey reached down and gave Dylan's head a pat. "Tenn knows what he's doing."

"It's getting too dangerous out here," Tenn decided. He

handed Billy da Pug to Casey and nudged Noah over. "Time to call it a day."

Dylan went to Tenn, got on his hind legs, and pawed the wheel. *Sumo needs help.*

"Sorry, Dylan. I'm a little busy here."

Me, too! Dylan flung his head back and howled.

Billy da Pug chimed in. *Heh, heh, heh.*

"What's the matter with Dylan," Noah asked.

"It's pretty choppy out here. Maybe he's getting seasick. Come here, Little Buddy."

"Everybody sit down," Tenn ordered. "You, too, Dylan."

Can't. Dylan ran to the back of the boat. He leaped onto the bench and stuck his head through the railing. *No Sumo.* He made his way to the back deck and searched the water. *Uh-oh.* Sumo was way behind them, one skinny arm barely holding his cell phone above the water.

You were right, Sumo. This boat really moves. Dylan's heart hammered in his chest as he watched Sumo getting smaller and smaller. He looked to Casey for help, but he was busy. *Time for me to move.*

Dylan jumped.

ELEVEN

Dylan belly-smacked the water and went under. *Yikes! The water is freezing!* His front and back paws kicked double-time and he struggled back to the surface. He started to arf! but it got stuck in his throat. *Too cold to arf.* He lifted his snout to the hot sun and sucked in warm air. *Ahh good.* Cold water ran from his topknot and into his eyes. *Not good.* Dylan gave a quick shake of his head sending his sopping mop flying away from his face. *Better.* Slowly he swam in a semicircle. *Sumo?*

"Here. I'm s-o-o c-old."

Dylan gave it all he had and dog-paddled hard. Or tried to. *My life jacket won't let me drown but it won't let me get to Sumo.* Dylan tried harder.

"That's it," Sumo coaxed through chattering teeth. "You're almost here."

I'm almost frozen. Dylan pushed himself forward in the water.

Sumo reached out and pulled him close.

Thanks! Dylan kicked back and felt the sunshine on his face. Opening his mouth wide, Dylan let a long sigh escape.

Sumo shoved his cell phone between Dylan's teeth. "Here."

Agh!

"Gotta keep my cell phone safe." Now Sumo sighed and rolled onto his back to float. The tips of his toes came above water. "I'm happy now."

I'm not. Dylan chomped on the cell phone a few times, trying to get it loose. *Ith sthuck in my mouth.* He tried moving it around with his tongue. *Really sthuck.*

"You're going to drop it!" Sumo jerked himself up. "Don't do that!"

Don't care. Ith making me drool.

"Look! A boat is coming." Sumo waved both arms over his head. "Over here!"

Dylan swung himself around and his life jacket smacked him in the chops. *That's Tenn's boat.* He saw Casey leaning over the railing, searching the water. *I knew you would come for me.*

"Dylan!" Casey called. "Dylan!"

Dylan's jaws clamped down hard on Sumo's cell phone and he tried bouncing in the water. *Here!*

"Do you think they see us?" Sumo was holding his life jacket away from his face with one hand and waving frantically with the other. "They gotta see us," he gasped. "They gotta get us." He held his hand out in front of him. "I'm so cold. My skin is turning blue."

I'm so cold and I can't feel my skin. Sumo's cell phone slid to the side of his mouth. Dylan bit down hard on it and heard a ping. *I hope I didn't break it.* Then he shook his head. *Too bad.*

"Dad!" Sumo shouted.

C'mon guys. Dylan saw Casey reach into his cargo shorts pocket and pull out his cell phone. Casey studied its screen, scanned the water, and shouted something to Tenn.

Tenn's boat picked up speed and aimed their way.

"They're coming! Yes!" Sumo shouted, "Over here!"

Tenn circled around them once, pulled alongside Sumo and Dylan and cut the boat's engine.

Sumo reached the boat first. "Thanks guys. I thought I was going to die out here."

"You could have." Tenn reached down and pulled him onto the boat. "Do you know how cold the lake is?"

I do! I do!

"Come here, Little Buddy." Casey was halfway down the ladder, holding onto it with one hand and motioning Dylan over with his other. "Get closer. You can do it."

Billy da Pug peered over the ladder and wagged his curly tail. *Heh, heh, heh.*

Three boats raced by. The lake rose and fell in their wake. A wave slammed over Dylan and sent a spray over Tenn, Noah, Billy da Pug, Sumo, and Casey. Billy da Pug skittered backward, away from the action.

I'm too cold to dog-paddle anymore. Dylan's front legs went limp. *Whine.*

"Dylan's too cold to swim." Noah leaned over the railing. "Give him to me."

Listen to Noah.

Casey slid into the water and hooked an arm around Dylan's middle. "You're okay now." Casey lifted him up. "Got him?"

Noah nodded.

"Here." Tenn tossed Noah a towel and dropped more on the deck.

Noah wrapped the towel around Dylan's head and body. "I'll rub you down, so you don't catch cold."

Too late. I'm already cold.

Noah dropped down beside Dylan on the deck and started drying him. Noah glanced at Sumo. "Everything was so crazy with the boat we didn't notice you were gone. Good thing you called Casey."

"Not me." Sumo showed his empty hands. "I gave Dylan my cell phone so it wouldn't get wet."

Dylan poked his face out of the towel, forced his cold jaws open and spit out the cell phone. It slid across the deck and stopped in front of Casey.

"Good job Dylan." Casey handed it to Sumo.

Thanks. Dylan worked his jaw left and right. *My mouth still works.*

Casey knelt in front of Dylan and brushed his topknot out of his eyes. "Why didn't you tell us Sumo was in the lake?"

I tried. Dylan sighed. *You never listen to me.* Dylan turned a little. *Rub my back Noah.*

"Good thing," Noah tossed Casey a towel, "Dylan's Dog Squad does search and rescue." Noah ruffled Dylan's ears and laughed. "Otherwise, Sumo would still be in the lake."

"Dylan can find anyone or anything. He has a great nose," Casey bragged and got to work on Dylan's other side. "He's found lost dogs, kids, and bad guys."

Just doing my job. Dylan raised his front paw to Noah. *Dry my paw.*

"Someday," Sumo added, "we're going to have a dog training school too. Casey will do the training and I'll handle social media. Thanks for saving my cell phone, Dylan."

Arf!

"You're lucky," Noah said. "You're already doing what you want to do."

"When I was a kid all I dreamed about was being a pro basketball player," Tenn admitted. "I was lucky. It happened for me. What about you?"

"Maybe a firefighter," Noah towel dried Dylan's ears, "or a pro basketball player."

"Do both," Tenn, Casey and Sumo said.

Arf! Dylan faced Noah and lifted his head up. *Don't forget my chest.*

Noah got the hint and rubbed. "Maybe." He kept his eyes down, not looking at Casey and Sumo. "There has only been one deaf firefighter and one pro deaf basketball player."

Casey tapped Noah on the shoulder. When he looked up, Casey said, "You got this. Dream big."

"Yeah," Noah laughed, "but it's kinda scary. What if I flop?"

Dreams are like sports. Unless you get out and play you got nothing to talk about later. Dylan licked Noah's face. *Don't forget my stomach.*

Tenn's cell phone pinged, and he read the screen. "Noah's mom has to work late. He's staying with us."

"Yes!" Casey, Sumo, and Noah fist bumped.

"I'll tell her you're broken-hearted." Tenn tapped the message into his cell phone and searched the sky. "It's getting late. Grab a dive bag and put all the wet towels in it. Then we need to get the boat in and pick up dinner."

"Barbecue!" Casey held up his hand and Dylan did a high four. "Yes!"

Noah got to his feet. "I want steak."

Me too!

"When do we eat?" Sumo rubbed his belly. "I'm starving."

You're always starving. Arf! Me too!

"Depends on how fast we get the boat in and pick up the chow."

"Great!" Sumo's face clouded over. "Hey, wait. I didn't get to drive the boat."

"That's because," Casey snorted and winged a wet towel at him, hitting him in the face, "Dylan was too busy saving you. Help me pick up the towels."

Dylan shook himself out. *I feel better now about the whole thing.* He spotted Billy da Pug curled up on a patch of sunlight and padded over. *Saving Sumo made me tired.* Dylan hunkered down next to the snoring pup and put his muzzle on his front paws. *Time for a nap.*

A few minutes later Dylan felt Tenn's boat change direction. *My nap was just getting good.* He nudged Billy da Pug awake. *We're here.*

The pup brought his wrinkled face close to Dylan's, snuffled once and went back to sleep.

"Guys get your gear." Tenn guided the boat into the dock slip.

"Jed's boat is gone." Sumo dumped the bag of wet towels near the ladder. "I didn't see him on the lake."

"It's a pretty big lake." Tenn cut the engine and secured the boat. He grabbed the bag of towels and waited for Casey, Dylan, Sumo, Noah, and Billy da Pug to get off.

When they walked up the ramp, music was softly drifting their way. By the time they passed the sandwich shop the music was blasting. A bluegrass band was playing energetically on the Lake Arrowhead Village stage. Between the stage and the parking lot, a plastic Slip and Slide with sprinklers and a pool had been set up.

There's got to be a zillion kids here.

A red-haired little girl in a bright pink and yellow bikini

elbowed an older boy in line for the Slip and Slide out of the way.

"I'm tellin' mom," he yelled in her face.

"So, what." She tossed up her arms, slid on her butt down the slide and landed in the pool. Jumping to her feet, she whirled around and stuck her tongue out at him. "Beat that meathead." Then she hopped back in line.

Dylan pawed Casey's leg. *Looks fun.*

"You just got dry." Casey tucked him under one arm. "I'll carry you to the Jeep. There are too many people here and you'll get stepped on."

"You too, Billy da Pug." Noah grabbed the pup around the middle and picked him up.

"How long does the Music Festival last," Sumo asked.

"Just for the weekend." Tenn slung the bag of towels over his shoulder. "Looks like a good turnout."

They threaded their way through the main parking lot dodging kids covered in face paint and parents pushing strollers. Determined visitors were double-parked in their cars hoping for a parking space.

"Uh, Tenn." Noah stopped at the back of the Jeep. "Somebody bashed in your bumper."

Ripped it off is more like it. Dylan studied the crumpled metal strip on the ground. *Whine.*

"That sucks." Sumo looked around. "Who did this? There has to be security cameras out here. We should call the sheriff."

"It's a busy day," Tenn cast a glance around the parking lot, "and accidents happen. Whoever did this is long gone."

"It's got to be Jed," Sumo said.

"Hold on." Tenn held up a hand. "We don't know that. I'm not accusing anyone if I'm not sure."

"Jed was pretty mad today. He threatened you," Casey

reminded him, "and when we got back to the dock his boat was gone."

"Casey's right," Noah nodded. "I bet it was him."

"Exactly," Sumo agreed. "Anyone else would've left a note or called you."

"How?" Tenn beeped the Jeep open. "They don't know my Jeep."

Casey pointed to the Jeep's license plate, Tenn 100. "Oh yeah?"

"Let's go." Tenn waved them inside. "I'll call it in later."

Casey opened the passenger door, put Dylan in his car seat and reached for his harness.

"Sit back and lift your muzzle."

Dylan leaned against the seat. Over Casey's shoulder he saw a tall man with a long black

braid standing next to a battered blue pickup truck. Dylan craned his neck up for a better look. *Jed's watching us.* Dylan saw him climb inside and drive off. *Grr.*

Casey ruffled Dylan's topknot "What's the matter?"

TWELVE

Tenn pressed the button to open the back of the Jeep. "Everyone grab a bag of groceries and take it to Mrs. Hudson. Then you can help her fix dinner."

"No way! There's a teepee in the backyard." Sumo pushed open his door. "Thanks Dad."

"Don't thank me." Tenn got out. "Thank Mrs. Hudson. It was her idea."

Noah was already out of the car and had his little dog clutched to his chest. "I gotta see this."

Noah, Billy da Pug and Sumo took off running.

Hurry! Dylan squirmed on his car seat. *We're getting left behind.*

"We're going to have so much fun tonight." Casey slung his backpack over his shoulder and helped Dylan out of the Jeep. "We'll stay up late and eat junk food until we barf."

I want to eat junk food. Dylan flicked his ears. *I don't want to barf.*

"Not so fast." Tenn held out a grocery bag to Casey. "Take this."

"And Little Buddy," Casey ignored Tenn, "Lake Arrowhead gets pretty cold at night, so we'll sleep in sleeping bags."

Dylan looked at the grocery bag Tenn was still holding. *I don't want to sleep in a bag.*

"Later Tenn. C'mon." Casey and Dylan raced off to the backyard. "I've never seen a teepee up close."

Oh wow. Dylan skidded to a stop beside Casey. *It's tall.*

Sumo pulled back the canvas flap and poked his head out. "This is so cool. When it gets dark, we can tell scary stories."

Dylan moved closer to Casey. *I don't want to be scared.*

Noah called, "We got cots with sleeping bags, a cooler full of soda and water, and a big screen TV. We're all set for the zombie movie marathon."

Any cookies? Dylan cocked his snout in the air and sniffed. *What about Cheetos? Cupcakes?*

"Here's the best part." Casey knelt beside Dylan and hugged him close. "Tenn has a firepit so we can make s'mores."

Great. Dylan nose-bumped Casey's nose. *Some more what?*

"S'mores are really yummy. The only problem is we have to wait until Tenn goes to bed. Then we'll sneak into the kitchen and get the stuff to make the s'mores. Adults get really crazy about kids messing around with fire."

Dylan rolled his eyes up to Casey's. *No kidding.*

"Are you coming?" Sumo stood back.

Casey and Dylan brushed past him and went inside. Three cots hugged the outline of the teepee forming a half circle. "Awesome."

Noah sat cross-legged on the middle cot beside his pup. "Billy da Pug already claimed this one."

"No worries." Casey dropped his backpack on the cot next to Noah's and sat down. "Hop up."

Okay. Dylan back kicked Casey's backpack to the dirt floor and trotted up and down on the sleeping bag. *I like this.* Dylan flopped down. When he punched out with his back paws, they hit the teepee. *This is one skinny bed.* Dylan ran his muzzle across Casey's lap and looked up. *I need to stretch out when I sleep. You can sleep on the ground.*

"We'll bring our stuff in later." Sumo went to the flap and waited. "Let's help Mrs. Hudson in the kitchen."

"Since when do you want to help?" Noah smirked.

Sumo rubbed his stomach. "Since I'm starving. She might feel sorry for us and give us a snack."

Dylan's stomach growled and he got to his paws. *Good idea Sumo. Let's go.*

They ran across the yard and over to the back door. Sumo started to yank the door open, but Casey put his hand on it, stopping him. He brought a finger to his lips, signing Quiet.

"What," Noah and Sumo mouthed.

Casey raised his right hand, curled down his third, fourth, and fifth fingers. He pointed his index finger straight up and his thumb pointed to his ear, signing Listen.

"This is serious." Mrs. Hudson's voice was fast and angry. "First someone tries to steal your horse. Poor Toby gets attacked, and now someone hits your Jeep. I'm telling you, Tennyson Stillwater, you've got trouble."

"Now, now," Tennyson began.

Mrs. Hudson switched to firm. "Don't you now me. You always see the good in people even when there isn't any. It's time you wake up and pay attention. My granny always said trouble comes in threes."

Tenn tried a laugh. "Then my troubles are over."

"None of your smart mouth," Mrs. Hudson warned. "Taking care of the ranch is your responsibility but taking care of you is my responsibility."

"Yes, ma'am."

"I'm glad we got that straight." Mrs. Hudson raised her voice, "Boys come in here. I've got work for you to do."

Yikes! Can she see us?

Casey turned to Sumo. "She's like psychic."

Dylan moved closer to Casey. *She's just like Mom.*

"Yup." Sumo shrugged and opened the door. "When do we eat?" He rose up on tiptoes trying to get a look at the kitchen counter behind her. "I don't want anything green. Especially kale. I hate kale."

"Kale is good for you." Tenn flashed them a wicked grin. "It's a summer favorite."

Noah made a face. "Oh gag."

"Kale's just plain nasty," Casey agreed. "Nuh-uh. Nothing green."

Dylan pawed Casey's leg. *What's kale?*

Mrs. Hudson tipped her head. "Grilled corn on the cob, baked potato with all the fixings, watermelon, deviled eggs, and cornbread. Steak, of course," she smiled, "because Noah is our guest and Dylan and Billy da Pug have a special diet."

Thanks Mrs. Hudson. Dylan waved his paw in the air. *I don't want anything nasty.*

"Thanks, Mrs. Hudson." Noah patted Billy da Pug's head and the pup licked his lips.

Sumo was on his toes again. "What about dessert?"

"Triple chocolate brownies."

"Ice cream," Noah asked hopefully.

"Nice try." Mrs. Hudson shook her head. "They had some at McDonald's."

Hardly any. We had to catch a bad guy.

"Boys, help Mrs. Hudson. I have to meet with Flynn Construction to go over the plans for the new dining hall." Tenn ran a hand through his hair. "It's been quite a day."

"The deputies are still investigating at the stables." Mrs. Hudson went to the fridge and pulled out potatoes. "So far they haven't found any clues."

"How do you know?" Tenn began and then put up both hands to stop her. "Never mind." He checked his cell phone. "I wish we'd hear something about Toby."

"He's still in a coma." Mrs. Hudson's voice softened. "You know his mother lives in Florida. She wanted to come but she just had knee surgery and can't fly. I promised to call as soon as we hear anything."

"Okay. I'll be back soon." Tenn pointed to Casey, Sumo, and Noah. "Do more than mooch while I'm gone."

Mooching is why we're here. Whine.

Mrs. Hudson zeroed in on their grubby hands. "Use the washroom off the kitchen to clean up and don't make a sloppy mess." She clapped her hands twice. "Hustle."

Casey motioned to Noah. "Follow me."

When they got to the washroom, Noah stopped and wrinkled his nose. "What smells?"

"Smells like," Sumo sucked in air, "cotton candy."

Dylan tested the air. *I like it. What's cotton candy?*

"Noah, you go first." Casey pointed to the sink. "Mrs. Hudson uses the smelliest soap. That's how she knows if we washed our hands."

After Noah washed his hands, he raised them to his nose. "Gross."

"Told you." Casey got busy but he didn't use any soap. When he finished, he wiped his hands on his cargo shorts.

"Not fair," Noah objected and reached for a hand towel. "You have to smell too."

"No way." Sumo laughed and ran his hands under the hot water. "You smell enough for all of us."

Noah laughed but sent the wet hand towel flying at Sumo.

Casey caught the towel, wadded it up and tossed it on top of the towel rack. It fell off and landed in a heap on the floor. "Seems strange the deputies are still at the stables." He looked at Noah. "Can you call your mom? Maybe they found something."

Look in your pocket, Casey. Whine.

"Nuh-uh." Noah shook his head hard. "Even if she knew she wouldn't tell. She can really keep a secret."

"It's been hours since Toby was hurt," Sumo folded his arms across his chest. "They found the shovel the guy used to hit him. What else do they need?"

Check out Casey's pocket. Hint, hint.

"My mom says some cases never get solved because they can't find enough evidence."

We've got evidence.

"I'm thinking," Casey said slowly and leaned back against the sink, "they can't find anything because it's already been found."

Good. Dylan shoulder-bumped Casey's leg. *Keep thinking.*

"Huh?" Sumo and Noah said.

"Dylan found this," Casey pulled the leather glove out of his cargo shorts pocket, "when he was in the stable. I put it in my pocket and forgot about it."

"It's a glove for the left hand," Noah said. "So what?"

"So, this morning," Sumo took it from Casey and ran his

fingers over the glove, "Fernando had gloves like this. I remember the ragged cuffs."

"Who is Fernando?" asked Noah.

Sumo filled him in. "Harry said he checked his references but something about the guy is off."

"Fernando got kinda mad when Sumo asked why he'd only be here a week," Casey added.

"You think Fernando hurt Toby?" Noah chewed on his lower lip. "Maybe I should call my mom."

Call Liz.

Casey shook his head slowly. "The glove could've been dropped any time."

"Or by anyone," Sumo said. "We need proof."

The glove belongs to Fernando. It has his smell.

"Sumo's right." Casey tossed up his hands. "All the ranch hands have leather gloves."

Dylan pawed Casey's leg. *It belongs to Fernando.*

"All ranch hands etch their initials inside." Sumo turned back the cuff on the glove and held it up. "FH. Fernando's last name is Huertas."

"Yes!" Noah grabbed the glove and looked it over. "I bet it's his."

"Boys," Mrs. Hudson called. "If you want to eat, you'd better get in here."

"We're coming," Sumo shouted back.

What about the glove?

"Don't say anything." Casey shoved the glove into his pocket. "We'll talk about this later."

You never listen to me. Dylan sighed and raced after Casey, Sumo, Noah, and Billy da Pug.

"Now what," Sumo asked Mrs. Hudson when they reached the kitchen.

"Clean the barbecue grill. The hammock hasn't been

used all summer. Wash it and hang it on the hammock hooks. Then scrub the picnic table and benches. The long white table will be perfect for serving so wash that too."

"Why?" Sumo grumbled. "We're eating outside. Who cares about a little dirt?"

I care about eating. Dylan stared up at Sumo. *Whine.*

"Sterling Ulysses Modragon," Mrs. Hudson stated flatly and then pointed to buckets, liquid detergent, scrub brushes and cleaning cloths. "You clean and you eat. Don't clean and you don't eat. Your choice."

Choose eating.

"This will take all day," Casey complained.

Dylan whipped his head around from Sumo and Casey to Mrs. Hudson. *Do it. Whine.*

Billy da Pug joined in. *Heh, heh, heh.*

Mrs. Hudson stood taller. "You're outvoted."

"Traitors," Casey muttered.

Dylan's stomach rumbled. *You'll thank me later.*

Noah grabbed a cleaning cloth and squirted some liquid detergent in a bucket. "The sooner we get started the sooner we'll eat."

"Smart boy." Mrs. Hudson's round face beamed.

They trooped outside and got to work.

There's nothing I can do to help. Dylan wandered over to where the hammock was puddled on the ground. *I wish it was hanging up. Hammocks are fun to swing in.* He scratched at the heavy cloth. *It's like the one we have at home.* Dylan jumped into the middle, used his front and back paws to scrunch the fabric together and collapsed on top of it. *Not bad.*

Billy da Pug waited near the picnic table. *Whine.*

Dylan cocked his head and panted. *Plenty of room.*

Billy da Pug bounded over and cuddled up next to Dylan.

You're a funny dog. Dylan licked the top of the little pup's head, and Billy da Pug settled down. *Don't snore.*

An hour later Dylan's nose twitched, and his lips quivered. *Something smells good.*

"Time to wake up," Casey coaxed and held out a treat.

Dylan opened one eye. *Goldfish crackers.* He took a nibble. *Dreaming about you working made me hungry. More please.*

"Hey," Noah called and waved the garden hose at Casey, "get back here and help me with the picnic table."

"I'm beat." Casey dropped down next to Dylan. "You got this."

A stream of cold water blasted over Casey, Dylan, and Billy da Pug. "Now *you* got this," Noah laughed.

Dylan and Billy da Pug scrambled back and shook the water off.

Casey jumped to his feet and Noah got him in the face with another, longer blast of water. "That does it," Casey sputtered but he was laughing. "You'd better start running."

"Look over here," Sumo had his cell phone up and video rolling. "You're soaked."

Behind him, Dylan heard the kitchen window slide open. *Uh-oh.*

"Great idea boys," Mrs. Hudson called cheerfully and tapped the dripping glass window. "You can wash the windows next."

THIRTEEN

"Steaks are ready," Tenn called. "Grab your plates and get in line."

"Excellent." Sumo got himself a paper plate. When Noah got two, Sumo elbowed him. "Billy da Pug gets his own plate?"

"Billy da Pug takes eating seriously." Noah held up an index finger sporting a striped Band-Aid. "He still has his baby teeth and they're really sharp."

Arf! Dylan smacked his paw on Casey's knee. *You heard Tenn. Grab our plates and I'll get in line.* Dylan trotted over to Tenn and sat.

Tenn used barbecue tongs to point to a sizzling steak. "Does Dylan like his steak medium?"

I like my steak in my stomach.

Casey tried nudging Dylan aside at the grill. "Yeah."

Hey! No cutting in line. Dylan dug in and stayed put. *I was here first.*

"Careful," Tenn warned. "It might be too hot for him."

Dylan watched the steak travel from the grill to the plate. *Mom touches it with her finger to make sure.*

Casey put his finger on the steak. "It's okay."

Thanks.

Tenn put a steak on Noah's plate. "Here you go."

"Looks good." Noah lowered the plate so Billy da Pug could see. "Hungry?"

Billy da Pug got up on his hind legs, gave the steak a good sniff, lost his balance and fell over backward. *Yip!* He rolled to his paws and shook himself out. *Heh, heh, heh.*

Sumo held his plate out. "I can't wait to eat." As soon as the steak hit his plate, he picked it up with his fingers and took a big bite.

Tenn snatched Sumo's steak with the barbecue tongs and put it back on the plate. "Wait until you get to the table."

"Why?" Sumo licked his fingers and ran his hand across his T-shirt leaving a smear. "I'm starving now."

"You're always starving," Casey insisted.

Noah laughed. "For a skinny kid you can really pack it away."

The best part is Sumo is a slob and drops most of it. I'm sitting next to him.

Tenn helped himself to the last steak. "Everything else is on the serving table."

Dylan raced ahead. He did a quick hop up and planted both front paws on the table. Shuffling along on his two back legs, he gave the food a good look. *All my favorites.* He shuffled back to Casey. *Get lots of everything.*

"Mrs. Hudson likes to feed us," Casey filled their plates, "so we'll get seconds."

And thirds. Dylan dropped down and trotted alongside Casey. *We don't want to disappoint Mrs. Hudson.*

"You got a lot done while I was gone." Tenn placed his

plate on the picnic table and sat down. "Did Mrs. Hudson threaten you with starvation?"

"Yeah." Casey reached for a bottle of water and filled Dylan's water dish. "But that's okay."

"We were happy to do it," Noah chimed in.

"Anything for Mrs. Hudson," Sumo mumbled through a mouthful of steak.

Tenn's fork stopped halfway to his mouth. Then he nodded. "I forgot. Triple chocolate brownies for dessert."

So, what? I don't get any. Dylan scratched at Casey's chair. *What about me?*

Casey broke off a chunk of cornbread and gave it to him.

"Thanks for letting me stay over." Noah spread butter on his corn on the cob. "Real food is so totally awesome. My mom can't cook. I bet Billy da Pug is the only dog that's never begged from the table." Red flashed across his face. "Don't tell her I said that okay?"

Tenn winked and cut into his steak. "Said what?"

"When will the dining hall be ready?" Sumo wiped his mouth with the hem of his T-shirt.

"Flynn promises by the end of summer." Tenn reached for their glasses and filled them with iced tea. "I'm planning a grand opening on Labor Day." He handed a glass to Noah. "By then the baseball diamond and bleachers will be finished."

"That's a lot to do." Casey cut Dylan's steak, added some plain baked potato, and put it down for him. "Here."

That's it? Dylan got on his hind legs and nose bumped Casey's plate. *Share the chow.*

Casey moved his plate out of reach.

Hey!

"Labor Day is way off." Sumo picked up a watermelon slice and bit in. "We should have a party or something now.

It would be fun." He waved the slice in the air and the slice broke in two.

Dylan caught the watermelon, and it disappeared in one gulp. *I love watermelon.*

"We'd help." Noah looked from Sumo to Casey. "Right guys?"

"Let me think about it," Tenn said slowly.

Sumo dropped the watermelon rind on his plate and spit out a seed. "That always means no."

"I didn't say no. Just let me think about it." Tenn started to take a drink but put the glass down. "A lot depends on what the deputies say. Toby is still in a coma." He took a deep breath. "This has been the longest day." Tenn checked his cell phone. "I wish we'd hear something."

The back door pushed open. Mrs. Hudson walked to them with a platter of brownies and gave the table a quick glance. "Need anything?"

"Everything is great. Thanks Mrs. Hudson." Tenn sent a look around the picnic table and cocked his head.

The boys got the hint. "Great."

"You're welcome. Finish your dinner," she set the platter of brownies in the middle of the table, "but save room for dessert."

What about me and Billy da Pug? Whine.

"Dogs can't have chocolate." Mrs. Hudson bent down and brushed Dylan's topknot out of his eyes. "Eating chocolate would make you very sick. You could even die."

I don't want to die. Dylan whined. *How about some cookies?*

Tenn's cell phone vibrated, and he read the caller ID. "It's Harry." He touched the screen. "You're on speaker. Any news?"

"I'm outside of Toby's room," Harry whispered. "I

heard the doctor say Toby is coming out of the coma. You said to let you know."

Tenn was already on his feet. "I'm leaving now." He closed the screen. "Sorry boys. Help Mrs. Hudson clean up after dinner." He shoved his cell phone into his jeans pocket. "Don't stay up too late. You're working in the old stable tomorrow morning."

"What!" Sumo stopped eating. "Why?"

Amazing. I've never seen Sumo stop eating before.

Casey groaned. "What time in the morning?"

"Five o'clock."

"It's dark at five o'clock," Casey protested. "The sun isn't up."

If the sun isn't up, it's nighttime. Dylan looked at Tenn. *I'm a dog and even I know that.*

"That sucks for you." Noah flashed a big grin. "Lucky me. I've got summer basketball practice."

"Yes," Tenn agreed, "but since you're sleeping over, your mom asked me to take you." Now he flashed a grin. "Practice isn't until seven a.m. so you'll have plenty of time to help."

"Yes!" Sumo and Casey chorused.

Noah wadded up his napkin and threw it at them. "Okay but I'm not cleaning any horse stalls."

"Mm-hmm." Mrs. Hudson picked up the platter of brownies and waited.

"Dude," Sumo warned.

Casey whispered, "We're talking triple chocolate brownies."

Noah hung his head. "Okay."

"I'll let you know when I hear anything." Tenn nodded to Mrs. Hudson. "Thanks."

Mrs. Hudson waved him off and checked her watch.

"Boys, I'm baking bread and need to get back to my kitchen." She gave them a stern look and shook a finger at them. "No brownies until you finish your dinner. Got it?"

"Yes, Mrs. Hudson."

Casey, Sumo, and Noah waited until she disappeared inside the house before attacking the brownies.

Arf! We were supposed to get seconds.

"Here you go." Casey gave Dylan a piece of cornbread.

Dylan chewed it open-mouthed and then dropped his paw on the rim of his empty water bowl, tipping it over. *Thirsty.*

"Sorry, Little Buddy." Casey filled it up.

Dylan finished off the water and went back to his empty dish. *Still hungry.* He sniffed around Casey's chair for crumbs. *Zip. But there's always Sumo.* Dylan found a corn cob by Sumo's foot. *It looks like a bumpy stick.* Dylan gave the corn cob a quick lick. *Oh boy. Lots of butter.* The corn cob rolled away but he snagged it with one paw and sank his jaws into it. *Ith stuck in my teeth.* Dylan dropped down and rolled with it. One fluffy ear wrapped around the cob. *Ith really stuck.* Dylan planted both paws on the corn cob and pulled back, yanking his ear free. *What's that smell?* He tipped his head and sniffed at the butter glob in his ear. *Flavor saver for later. Yum.*

Dylan wandered over to Noah's chair. Billy da Pug was passed out on his back next to his clean plate. His tan round belly and his four sturdy legs were sticking straight up. *You look like a baked potato with legs.*

"That's good news about Toby waking up," Sumo said.

The bad news is I could starve. A gentle breeze brought food smells Dylan's way. *Steak!* He went to Tenn's empty seat and scented the air again. *Tenn didn't get to finish his dinner. Too bad for him. Good for me.* Dylan looked up at

Casey. *You're talking and not paying attention to me. That's rude.* Dylan hopped quietly onto Tenn's chair and hunkered low until his eyes were table high. *I can see and not be seen.*

Casey waited for Noah to look at him. "What's going to happen when Toby wakes up?"

"The deputies will ask him what he remembers."

Dylan slowly brought his head up to the plate. *Yay! Tenn cut up his steak.* A few licks later, the steak had disappeared. He sniffed at Tenn's baked potato but turned up his nose. *No butter.*

"That's so cool." Sumo got excited. "When Toby wakes up, he'll finger the bad guy. The deputies will arrest him and grill him for like a hundred hours. Then they'll throw him in jail where he'll rot in a dark cell with bad plumbing and have only rats for company and eat nothing but stale bread and lime Jell-O for the rest of his miserable life."

"Whoa! I can't read lips that fast." Noah looked to Casey. "What came after bad guy?"

"Sumo watches too much TV." Casey rolled his eyes but repeated what Sumo had said. "You know," Casey added slowly, "it might be better for Toby if he doesn't remember."

"Yeah." Noah broke a brownie in two and stuffed half into his mouth. "If the bad guy thinks Toby can identify him, Toby won't be safe. The bad guy will want to shut him up for good."

That's what bad guys do. Dylan went back to Tenn's plate. *No cornbread. No watermelon. Bummer.*

"What about all the other stuff that happened today? My dad has never hurt anyone."

Casey frowned and toyed with his iced tea glass. "None of this adds up."

"My mom's been a detective a long time. She says when things don't add up, find out what they all have in common." Noah hunched forward and put his elbows on the table. "Start from the beginning."

Now Casey and Sumo put their elbows on the table and hunched forward.

"Everything was okay until Dad won Nell and the horse trailer from Mr. Tompkins in a blackjack game. Mr. Tompkins was a sore loser and shot at Dad. He missed and hit the horse trailer. Later Ronny tried to steal Nell."

Keep talking. Don't pay attention to me. Dylan found a slice of avocado. *My favorite.*

"Toby was attacked in the stable," Casey continued, "but that can't have anything to do with Mr. Tompkins and Ronny. They don't know him."

"Jed had to be the one who wrecked Dad's bumper. He was at the lake when we were and was pretty mad about the sports ranch."

Noah shook his head. "We don't know if he was anywhere near the ranch when Toby was hurt."

"Maybe," Casey reasoned, "none of this has anything to do with Tenn or Toby or the sports ranch. Maybe it has to do with something in the stable."

"Nuh-uh. The horses are all rescues." Sumo wiped his hands on his shorts. "None of them are valuable."

"What about Fernando?" Casey pushed his plate away. "He just happens to get hired the same day Toby gets hurt and he has gloves with ragged cuffs."

Fernando dropped one in the stable. Dylan started to eat a pickle but changed his mind. *Tastes funny.*

Casey leaned closer. "Dylan found a left-handed glove with a ragged cuff at the stable."

Dylan ate a square of white cheese. *The glove is Fernando's. His smell is on it.*

"Big deal." Noah brushed it off. "You said everyone on the ranch has gloves like that."

"But not with a ragged cuff," Sumo argued, "and the initials FH etched inside."

Dylan teased a tomato slice off the plate and ate it.

Casey scrubbed his hands over his face. "None of this makes sense."

It doesn't make sense we didn't get seconds. Dylan studied Tenn's plate. *One deviled egg left.* He leaned forward and nipped. The deviled egg flew off the plate, hit Casey on the arm and landed in the grass.

"Dylan!" Casey swiped at the egg on his arm. "You ate Tenn's dinner!"

Dylan sat up straight. *It was abandoned.*

"Your face and ears are a mess." Casey grabbed a napkin and tried to run it over Dylan's ear. "You got butter in your ears."

Don't! Dylan squirmed away from Casey. *It's a flavor saver.* He angled his head and licked at the chunk of butter. *Yum.*

"Look over here." Sumo waved his cell phone at Dylan. "Dylan's Dog Squad fans want to see you at a barbecue."

Noah was cracking up. "Is Dylan allowed to sit at the table?"

Dylan sat up straighter. *There was a vacancy.*

"Nuh-uh." Casey helped him down. "You know the rules."

The rules stink. Dylan waited for Casey to look away before he pounced on the deviled egg. *Good stuff.*

"It's getting dark." Sumo checked his cell phone. "Zombie movie marathon is about to start."

"We're watching it in the teepee, right?" Noah reached for the brownie platter.

"Oh yeah." Casey picked up their plates and balanced Dylan's water dish on top. "Then it'll be super scary."

"It's so cool when zombies eat people." Sumo made loud gnawing noises and smacked his lips. "The first movie I saw gave me nightmares for a week."

I don't like scary. Dylan leaned against Casey's leg. *I don't want the zombies to eat me. I don't want nightmares. What are they?*

"It's okay, Little Buddy. I'll keep you safe."

Thanks, Casey. You're the best.

FOURTEEN

You're in really big trouble. Dylan covered his eyes with both paws. *I can't look.* He lowered one paw and peeked at the young barefoot girl in a long white dress on TV. *Get out of there.*

A crash happened off screen and the girl whirled around.

The zombies are coming!

Her scream split the night.

Run! Dylan bunched his legs under himself and leaned forward. *Don't look back.*

Creepy background music started low and ramped up. Dylan stayed glued to the TV. *A road is over there. Woods are in front of you.* Dylan shivered. *Never go into the woods!*

She ran into the woods.

Ugh!

In seconds she was fighting her way through a tangle of brush and trees.

Told you!

Branches tore at her arms and rough ground cut her feet. She left a bloody trail as she ran deeper into the woods.

Zombies can smell blood. Run faster!

The moon came up, round and waxy, casting shadows below. Panting hard the girl clutched her side and slowed to a limp.

Are you nuts? Keep going!

A six-foot-tall zombie stepped from the shadows and caught the girl by the throat.

Yikes!

The zombie lifted her off the ground and brought her terrified face to his.

Scream for help!

She screamed but the zombie's long bony fingers slowly squeezed her throat hard, harder, and harder still. Her scream ended in a gurgle and her eyes rolled back into her head. One tiny hand fluttered in the air before she went limp. The zombie dropped her, howled up at the moon and sank his white pointy fangs into her flesh.

Agh! Dylan shut his eyes. *Nobody ever listens to me.*

"It's okay, Little Buddy." Casey pulled him close. "You can look now."

Dylan let out a shuddering breath and watched the movie credits roll on the TV screen. *That was so scary. The zombies ate everyone.* His stomach pitched. *I'll never ever eat anything ever again.*

Sumo tossed the TV remote aside, got up and poked his head outside the teepee. "The house lights are off. Mrs. Hudson must be asleep." He rubbed his hands together. "S'mores time!"

"I don't know." Casey rubbed Dylan's shoulders. "The zombie movies were pretty scary. Dylan might be too upset to eat."

Are you crazy? Dylan jumped off the cot. *S'mores time!*

"What if Tenn comes back?" Noah asked.

"Dad sent a text when we were watching the movie. The doctors are still with Toby." Sumo checked the time. "We'll hurry."

Noah softly stroked Billy da Pug's head and whispered, "Wake up." The pup yawned, unfurled his pink tongue, and rolled over to his stomach.

"We got to be really quiet," Sumo said. "If Mrs. Hudson hears us, she'll get all snoopy."

"Don't turn the lights on in the house." Casey brought out his cell phone. "Use your flashlight app."

"Okay." Noah turned his on.

"Wait." Casey crouched and put his finger to his lips, signing Quiet to Dylan.

Noah did the same with Billy da Pug.

"Follow me." Sumo held the flap of the teepee open for them. "I know where everything is."

They crept across the lawn and up the back steps. Sumo put his ear to the door, waited and then turned the handle. They stepped inside. Sumo went to the pantry and handed marshmallows, chocolate bars and graham cracker packages to Casey. In the kitchen Sumo opened drawers until he found the marshmallow skewers and gave them to Noah. When he pushed the drawer in it scraped on its runners.

Sumo, Casey, and Noah jumped.

Yikes!

"Run," Sumo hissed.

Noah and Billy da Pug were already out the door. Casey, Dylan, and Sumo scrambled over themselves and raced across the lawn. They pushed their way into the teepee and fell onto their cots laughing.

"That was awesome." Sumo sat up. "I can't believe Mrs. Hudson didn't hear us."

"Oh, man. We didn't get any paper plates to put the

s'mores on." Casey tore open a graham cracker package and lined up the graham crackers on his sleeping bag. He broke the chocolate bar into small squares and put them on the crackers. "We'll have to carry them outside."

Sumo got up. "Hurry up. I'm going to light the firepit."

"Okay." Noah started putting marshmallows on the skewers. "I haven't had s'mores since last summer."

I haven't had them ever. Dylan rested his muzzle on Casey's cot for a better look. *Hint, hint.*

Casey broke a graham cracker in two and gave half to Dylan. "Can Billy da Pug have this?"

Billy da Pug raked his sharp nails down Casey's bare leg. *Heh, heh, heh.*

"Ouch!" Casey gave Billy da Pug the cracker. "That would be a yes."

"He's the shy type." Noah gave a half laugh and put the last marshmallow on the skewer.

"Wait a second." Casey rummaged through Sumo's backpack and found his iPad. "We can use this like a tray to carry them out." Casey moved the s'mores to the iPad and tucked the graham cracker package under his arm.

"Where's the firepit?" Noah turned on his flashlight app, stuck his cell phone between his teeth and picked up the marshmallow skewers.

"This way."

Dylan saw the fire burning bright against the dark night and took off. Billy da Pug raced alongside him.

"Is that my iPad?" Sumo pointed to Casey's hands. "There better not be any crumbs in the keyboard."

"Relax." Casey set the iPad on the edge of the firepit. "We'll eat them fast."

"You moron! Never put an iPad near fire!" Sumo yanked the iPad away and the s'mores flew off.

Dylan and Billy da Pug dove for the food.

"You're the moron!" Noah held Dylan and Billy da Pug back so Casey could pick up the s'mores. "Dogs can't have chocolate."

"Relax," Casey said again. He set the graham crackers on the edge of the firepit and put the chocolate pieces on top. "There." He flicked off a twig. The dirt stayed. "We're all good."

"Okay," Sumo said grudgingly and grabbed a marshmallow skewer from Noah. "The fire is hot. Let's toast the marshmallows."

Noah wadded up his sweatshirt and tossed it onto a camp chair. He made a face and jerked a thumb over his shoulder. "I got to go pee."

Casey put his hands on his hips. "Why didn't you go when we were inside?"

"I didn't have to go then."

Sumo waved his marshmallow skewer toward the trees. "Go in the woods."

"No way." Noah took a step back. "Animals are in the woods."

And zombies.

"I'll be really fast." Noah turned on his flashlight app. "Take care of Billy da Pug."

"Sure." Casey pulled two camp chairs close to the firepit and waited for Dylan to hop up. He patted the seat of the other chair and Billy da Pug jumped onto it. "You can watch."

Front row seat. Dylan gave the firepit his full attention. *Like it!*

Billy da Pug put his muzzle on his front paws and kept his little eyes fixed on Casey.

"I like my marshmallows really gooey." Sumo stuck his

skewer into the flame and his marshmallow blazed.

I don't think gooey means what you think it means. Dylan watched gray smoke spiral upward into the black night. *The marshmallow is on fire.*

"You and Billy da Pug are getting special s'mores. No chocolate." Casey kept the skewer above the fire. "I'll cook the marshmallows just enough, so they melt and stick to the graham crackers."

Dylan hooked his front paws over the edge of the camp chair and watched Casey rotate the skewer. Slowly the marshmallow turned golden brown and sugary smells filled the night air. Dylan's nose quivered and he wiggled his buns. *Whine.*

"Done!" Sumo put the marshmallow on the graham cracker with the chocolate square, covered it with another graham cracker and pulled the skewer free. He smooshed the graham crackers together and took a big bite. "Oh! Ow! Agh!" His eyes popped and he fanned his mouth with his free hand. "That's *hot*."

That's dumb. Dylan flicked his ears left and right. *It was on fire.*

Sumo blew on the s'more and used his fingertips to break it in half. Marshmallow and chocolate oozed out. He opened his mouth wide and dropped it in. "Ow! It's still hot."

You just don't learn. Dylan started to whine but kept it to himself.

"But," Sumo chewed fast, "it's good." He swallowed and wiped his mouth with the hem of his T-shirt. "What's taking Noah so long?"

"Who knows?" Casey touched the marshmallow with this finger and showed it to Dylan. "Just right." He made the s'more and broke it in two. "Half for you, Little Buddy."

Dylan jumped down from the chair and took it in one gulp. He licked his muzzle and shoulder bumped Casey's leg. *Good.*

Heh, heh, heh. Billy da Pug wiggled on the camp chair.

"I know you want this," Casey looked from the pup to the house, "but I don't know how much you can have."

Suddenly the house hallway light came on.

"No, no, no," Sumo moaned. "It's Mrs. Hudson!"

"This is so bad." Casey gave the s'more half to Billy da Pug. "Get out of there, Noah."

The back door opened, and Noah softly closed it behind him.

Yay!

Noah stumbled and took a header off the steps, landing hard on the grass.

Ouch!

Noah got to his knees. A second later he was up and shaking out his hands.

Whew!

The kitchen light came on. Through the window they saw Mrs. Hudson go to the back door, lock it, and turn off the outside light. She glanced around the kitchen before turning off the light.

Dylan huffed out a sigh. *That was close.*

Casey and Sumo turned to each other. "Yes!"

Uh, guys. Dylan searched the yard. *Where's Noah?*

"Wait." Casey squinted into darkness. "Noah's gone."

Sumo did a one-eighty. "He was here."

"I'm going after him." Casey grabbed his cell phone and turned on the flashlight app. "It's pitch black out there. He must've gone the wrong way."

"If he gets lost in the woods," Sumo's voice trailed off.

"I'm coming, too." He turned off the firepit. "What about Billy da Pug?"

"I don't see his leash. He'll have to stay here." Casey broke a graham cracker in two and gave it to the pup. "We don't want to lose him. This will keep him busy until we get back."

"The upstairs windows are open." Sumo pointed to the house. "If Billy da Pug barks Mrs. Hudson will hear him."

"You're right." Casey broke two more graham crackers into pieces and gave them to Billy da Pug. "If he's eating, he won't be barking."

"We need to get started." Sumo scanned the dark night. "Noah could be anywhere."

He must be so scared.

"I'm texting him," Casey's thumbs flew over his cell phone screen, "and telling him we're coming and to stay where he is." Casey held both arms out to Dylan and tapped his right fist on his left wrist, signing Work.

Let's go.

Casey picked up Noah's sweatshirt and gave Dylan the scent. "This is Noah. Dylan, find Noah."

Got it! Dylan started to arf.

Casey put his index finger to his lips, signing Quiet.

Oh yeah. Dylan trotted across the lawn and sniffed around the steps. Then he raised his head and scented the air.

Casey gave him Noah's sweatshirt again. "This is Noah. Dylan, find Noah."

Dylan put his nose to the ground. *Noah went into the woods.* Dylan looked up at Casey and whined. *Not good. Zombies are in the woods.*

"Dylan, find Noah."

Okay. Okay. Keeping his nose to the ground Dylan

headed for the woods and picked his way across pine needles. At a pine tree he stopped, sat, and alerted. *Arf!*

"Dylan found something." Casey hustled over. "Good boy."

Dylan alerted again. *Arf!*

"Uh-oh." Sumo picked up Noah's cell phone. "This is bad. Noah doesn't know we're looking for him."

Really bad. Noah can't see in the dark without his flashlight app.

"Do this." Casey held up his cell phone, sending a beam of light into the woods. "Maybe he'll see our light and shout or something."

Dylan circled the pine tree and sniffed the ground. *Lots of smells here.* Dylan's ears pricked and he froze. *Zombies? Grr.*

"What is it, Little Buddy?"

Whine. Dylan scented the air again. *Noah isn't alone.*

Casey gave Dylan the sweatshirt again. "This is Noah." Casey shined his light ahead. "Dylan, find Noah."

I hear someone running. Dylan cut through trees and leaped over a fallen log. *This way guys.*

Casey and Sumo followed close behind Dylan, lighting the way.

"Look," Sumo shouted. "There!"

In the clearing Noah was bent over at the waist and breathing hard.

Dylan ran to him and jumped up, planting both front paws on his thighs. *Arf! Arf!*

"Dylan!" Noah dropped to his knees and buried his face in Dylan's neck. "You found me!"

Arf!

Casey jogged over and waited until Noah looked up. "I told you Dylan has a great nose."

Noah touched his fingertips to his lips and then moved them slightly down and toward Dylan, signing Thank You.

Just doing my job!

"What happened?" Sumo handed Noah his cell phone. "Why did you run?"

"I wanted to bring the leftover brownies back with me and went into the kitchen. All of a sudden, the hallway light switched on. I thought Mrs. Hudson would catch me so I took off."

"We saw you fall down the stairs." Casey laughed. "That had to hurt."

"No joke." Noah stood up and brushed pine needles off his knees. "I was so scared I ran the wrong way and ended up in the woods. Then," Noah shuddered, "some guy grabbed me. That's when I lost my cell phone. I took off running again."

"Did you see him?" Sumo demanded.

"It was too dark." Noah hesitated. "But when he grabbed me, he said something to me."

Sumo frowned. "How do you know?"

"His mouth was close to my ear, and I could feel his breath. When people talk their breath comes out kinda uneven. His breath was really fast. Like he was angry. Then he pushed me down." Noah held up his cut and bleeding hands.

"Do you remember anything else about this guy?" Casey asked.

"Yeah. When he grabbed me, he covered my mouth with his right hand. He was wearing a glove. I know because I bit him. He wasn't wearing a glove on his left hand. I felt his fingers digging into my arm."

"Fernando lost his left glove," Sumo said. "It had to be him."

Casey studied the woods. "What if he's still here? He could be watching us."

Dylan moved closer to Casey. *Whine.*

"This is all so weird." Noah shivered and rubbed his bare arms. "First Toby and now me."

"Fernando is mixed up in this." Casey tossed Noah his sweatshirt. "It's time we found out why."

"It's time Fernando finds out he can't mess with any of us." Sumo stuck out his chin. "Dylan's Dog Squad is officially on the case."

"Thanks guys." Noah pulled his sweatshirt over his head.

You bet! We're a team.

"No way Fernando's getting away with this." Casey pointed to Dylan and Sumo. "We're in this together. All we need is a plan to catch him."

Arf! Dylan swung his head from Casey to Noah and Sumo. *What is it?*

"We'll sneak into the bunkhouse and go through his stuff," Casey said slowly.

"Fernando's leather glove will have bite marks on it. That's evidence." Noah got excited. "Then we could tell my mom. She'd know what to do."

"His glove would only prove he attacked *you, not* Toby." Casey shook his head. "We need more."

We need a better plan.

"We need to find evidence that he's working for Mr. Tompkins." Casey chewed on his lower lip. "Let's go to the bunkhouse tonight. We won't get caught because all the ranch hands will be asleep."

Uh. Dylan body bumped Casey. *Your plan doesn't make sense.*

"I'm in." Sumo's cell phone vibrated. He read the screen

and freaked. "Dad just left the hospital!" He shoved his cell phone back into his pocket. "We got fifteen minutes to get back, clean up the mess at the firepit and get into bed before he gets home. If we don't, we're dead."

"What about Fernando?" Casey argued. "What about our plan?"

"Tomorrow!" Sumo grabbed Noah's arm and started running to the woods.

Dylan shot off after them. *You're on your own.*

"Dylan!"

I don't want to be dead.

FIFTEEN

Casey unzipped the screen on Dylan's bike trailer and poked his head in. "You've got to get out and walk."

Dylan pivoted on his buns and stared out the side screen. *No.*

"These hills are too steep. I can't peddle anymore."

So, your problem is my problem?

"You're pouting."

Am not. Dylan spared Casey a glance. *Maybe just a little.*

"We're almost to the old stable. You can do this."

It's too early. Dylan gave a jaw cracking yawn and stepped out one paw at a time. He stretched himself forward on his front legs and then stretched himself backward. His rump collapsed on his comfy cushion and stayed there. *I like my ride.*

"Please."

Dylan gave Casey a big, brown-eyed stare. *What's in this for me?*

Casey shrugged off his backpack and rifled around

inside. "Mrs. Hudson made cookies." He found the treat bag, then broke a cookie into pieces and held one out.

What kind? Dylan stayed put, but he leaned forward and took the cookie with his front teeth. *Peanut butter. Not bad.*

Casey ruffled Dylan's topknot and helped him out. "We need to hurry so we can catch up to Noah and Sumo."

Dylan padded alongside Casey. His paws sent up dirt puffs. *It's hot. Grr.* Dylan cut in front of Casey's bike.

"Careful, Little Buddy. I nearly ran you over." Casey stopped to wipe his damp palms on his shorts before gripping the handlebars again. "C'mon."

Dylan sat down. *Carry me.*

"Nice try. We're walking." Casey pushed his bike along the path until they reached Sumo and Noah. "Sun is up."

"Big wow. So are we." Sumo leaned on his handlebars and trudged along. "If we'd gone the long way to the old stable, we could've ridden our bikes the whole way."

You could've thought of that first. Dylan watched Billy da Pug darting in and out of bushes chasing white butterflies. *Walking uphill is nuts.*

"At least Tenn let me borrow his bike," Noah mumbled. "Riding part of the way is better than nothing. I can't believe it's so early."

"I thought he was kidding about getting up at five." Casey brushed his hair out of his eyes. "Good thing Mrs. Hudson took pity on us and made breakfast."

The pancakes were really yummy. Dylan sighed happily. *The scrambled eggs were fluffy but not as good as Mom's.* Dylan's tongue dribbled little drips on the dirt path. *My mouth is leaking.*

"We're here." Casey steered his bike over to the side of the old stable and hung his helmet on the handlebars. He got a bottle of water and Dylan's collapsible dish out of his backpack and started to pour. "Thirsty?"

Dylan didn't wait for Casey to finish pouring but dove in and drank nonstop. *Thanks.*

Casey showed the water bottle to Noah. "Does Billy da Pug want some?"

"Maybe." Noah looked around and called, "Billy da Pug!"

Billy da Pug came out of the bushes, dragging a big stick behind him in the dirt.

"That's some stick." Sumo yanked off his helmet and ran a hand through his hair.

"We buy him toys, but he goes for the sticks every time. He has a stack of them at home." Noah showed Billy da Pug the water dish. "Want some?"

The pup eyed it but refused to give up the stick.

Noah gave the dish back to Casey. "Guess not."

A burst of loud long screeches followed by short ones came from the old stable.

Agh! Dylan dropped to the ground and pawed his ears.

"No," Sumo moaned and gritted his teeth. "I can't believe Keegan is still learning to play the Irish fiddle."

Keegan still needs more lessons.

The stable door opened and a young guy with hair the color of a stop sign ambled out carrying an Irish fiddle.

"Sounds..." Casey gave Keegan a thumbs up and struggled for a word, "great."

Sounds awful.

Keegan blushed as red as his hair and gave his fiddle a light pat. "Thanks. My dream is to play in an Irish band."

Dylan shook his ears out. *Dream about something else.*

Sumo pulled the stable door open, and Casey, Dylan,

and Noah went in first. Billy da Pug came along, dragging his stick.

It's cool inside. Dylan shook his damp topknot out of his eyes. *Much better.*

Soft morning sunlight filtered in and bathed everything in gold. Hopeful horses trotted forward and hung their faces over the railing for attention. Whinnies and snorts greeted them when they walked past.

Hi to you, too!

"The stable is really old and really big." Noah sucked in air. "Smells like horses and hay."

No kidding. Achoo! Dylan's eyes watered and he hauled back his head and sneezed again. *Why is there so much hay?*

"Guys?" Tenn called. "I'm in Ebony's stall." Tenn brought her to the railing, set the grooming bucket down, and tossed in the curry brush. Ebony poked her nose through the railings toward Sumo.

"Hey Ebony." Sumo stroked her nose. "You look good."

"I always groom Ebony myself." Tenn gave her an alfalfa and molasses treat from his jeans pocket. "She likes to look her best."

Ebony looks like a shaggy black dog with really long white whiskers.

Casey picked Dylan up and brought him nose-to-nose with her. "Ebony is a pony."

Oh. Dylan looked up at Casey. *What's a pony?*

"A pony is a little horse that will never get any bigger."

I won't get any bigger. What's wrong with that?

Noah reached through the railing and Ebony snuffled his hand. "She's so calm."

"Dad let me ride her when I was a little kid. I had to stop when I got too big."

Tenn stroked Ebony's mane. "When I moved to Lake

Arrowhead there was a guy with a ranch on the other side of the lake. He had a bunch of ponies and on weekends he gave pony rides. He didn't want Ebony anymore because she was too old." Tenn tickled her ear. "She was twenty-two when I bought her and she's thirty now." Tenn tickled her other ear. "She's a granny."

I'm glad Ebony has a nice life now. Dylan licked Casey's cheek. *What's a granny?*

A loud snort and the stomping of hooves had them turning around.

Nell! Dylan wiggled in Casey's arms. *Let me down.*

"Stay still," Casey whispered. "Nell's ears are back. That means she's upset." Casey put his finger to his lips, signing Quiet.

"Easy girl." Harry was struggling to walk Nell on a lead rope toward Tenn.

Nell wasn't having it. With every step she jerked back on the lead rope and shook her head. Her dark eyes darted wildly around the stable.

"Will walked her earlier." Tenn kept his voice low. "He said she was fine."

"She'll settle down." Harry tightened his grip on the lead rope. "There, there," he soothed, and ran his hand along her neck. "Where do you want her?"

Nell quivered and sidestepped narrowly missing Harry's cowboy boots.

Something is wrong with Nell.

Tenn jutted his chin to an empty stall. "Next to Ebony."

Ebony body-bumped Tenn, knocking him off balance.

"Jealous?" Tenn teased. "You'll always be my best girl." He offered her an alfalfa and molasses treat from his jeans pocket. She drew back her lips and took it from his open palm.

Dylan forgot about being quiet. *Arf!*

Nell's head whipped around. When she found Dylan, her dark eyes calmed and stayed on him. She blew air through her nose and two-stepped in place.

"Sumo," Tenn said softly, "open the gate. Casey, go into the stall with Dylan. Let's see if Nell will follow you inside."

"Okay." Casey waited for Sumo to open the gate. Holding Dylan close, Casey walked to the center of the stall.

Nell threw up her head and whinnied happily. She lunged forward, dragging Harry into the stall with her.

Dylan one-pawed the air. *You're okay now. I'm here.*

Casey put Dylan down. "Wait for Nell to come to you."

Whine.

Nell stepped forward, brought her head down to Dylan's and nuzzled him.

It's me. Dylan wagged himself all over and licked her nose. *Hi.*

Nell returned the lick, knocking Dylan on his butt.

Hey! Dylan scrambled to his paws and swiped at his wet face. *That was one big sloppy kiss.* He gave Nell a happy grin. *Thanks!*

"She's all yours." Harry handed Casey the lead rope.

"Okay."

"Nell's calm now but wait a while before you groom her. I want to make sure she stays that way." Tenn went in and gave Casey the grooming bucket. Then he motioned Sumo and Noah in. "Sumo you'll start with Rocket. After you groom all the horses, you can clean their water dishes."

"Dad," griped Sumo. "You said we'd go riding today."

Tenn ignored him. "Then you can clean the stalls."

"This is a horse-*riding* ranch," Casey grumbled. "When do we get to the riding part?"

You promised I could go riding. Whine.

"Tenn Hundred Acres is a *working* horse ranch," Tenn corrected. "That means everybody works." He smiled. "Get your work done and then you can go riding. Did you bring the backpack for Dylan?"

"It's rolled up in his bike trailer."

Arf! I get to go.

"What about me?" Noah asked.

"I'll take you to practice in an hour. You can help Sumo and Casey until then."

Noah crossed his arms over his chest. "I want to ride the horses, too."

"You're invited here any time."

"It's not the same. I want to go riding today." Noah turned his back on Tenn. "This stinks. Casey and Sumo get to go."

Tenn put a hand on Noah's shoulder and waited for him to turn around. "Your mom gave me strict orders to get you to practice." He tipped his head. "She caught a robbery case this morning and thinks it will take a while. If she's still on it when practice is over, you can come back."

"Yeah, yeah."

Casey got Noah's attention. "All this horse stuff will take forever. I'll text you when we're done. We'll go riding then."

"Really?" Noah perked up and looked at Sumo.

"Yeah, really," Sumo agreed. "Dylan's Dog Squad has things to do."

"Like what? Dylan's Dog Squad does search and rescue." Tenn's dark eyes went from Sumo to Casey to Noah. "What's going on here?"

Sumo said sweetly, "Noah is Dylan's Dog Squad's newest friend."

"My mom likes it when I make new friends," Noah added. "Billy da Pug needs training and Casey promised to help."

Casey jumped in. "Absolutely. It's what friends do."

You left out the part about going after Fernando.

"Really?" Tenn waited a beat but let it go. He pointed to a black horse with a white blaze on its face. "Noah ,you can groom the Empire."

Noah's mouth dropped open. "That horse is like ten feet tall. I'll need a stepladder to reach his mane."

"That's why he's named Empire," Sumo snickered.

"The Empire State Building is in New York City," Casey told Dylan. "It's one thousand two hundred fifty feet tall."

That's a lot.

"Good idea," Tenn agreed. "There's a stepladder in the tack room. You can get it when you get the grooming buckets."

"You're lucky." Casey gave Noah a friendly punch on the arm. "By the time you finish grooming Empire, it will be time for you to go to practice. We're stuck doing everything else."

"Get to work." Tenn clapped his hands together. "I've got things to do but I'll be back in an hour."

"Before you go," Harry cleared his throat, "any news about Toby?"

"He's out of the coma. He doesn't remember anything, but the doctor thinks his memory will come back." Tenn checked the time. "After I take Noah to practice, I'm going to the hospital. You should go too."

"Can't. I need to train the new ranch hands."

"We won't stay long." Tenn reached into his pocket and came up empty. "Harry, give some treats to Casey." He winked at Casey. "Treats always make grooming easier."

Harry got the treats out of his pocket. When he started to hand them to Casey, Nell

flattened her ears and backed into a corner.

"Nell doesn't like you," Sumo blurted out and laughed.

"Sumo," Tenn warned.

"Sorry." Sumo laughed again. "Maybe she's afraid of Harry's bald head."

It is really shiny. Harry must be cold when the wind blows. Dylan shook out his fluffy topknot and ears. *I'm never cold.* Dylan moved closer to Nell. *Don't be afraid. I'll stay with you.*

"Easy girl." Harry held out the treats again. "I'm not taking you away from Dylan."

"When Nell and Dylan met," Casey slipped the treats into his pocket, "it was instant friendship."

Nell is my friend.

"No worries." Harry brushed it off. "Sumo. Noah. I'll show you where everything is in the tack room."

Noah looped Billy da Pug's leash around the lowest railing of Ebony's stall. "Stay here."

Billy da Pug looked up for a second and then went back to chewing on his stick.

Tenn's cell phone pinged, and he glanced at the screen. "Hold on, Noah." Tenn read the text and looked up. "Your mom says your basketball coach has a cold and practice is canceled."

"Yes!" Noah gave a thumbs up.

Tenn smiled but kept his tone serious. "You have a choice. Do you want to go to your grandparents, or do you want to stay here?"

"Duh."

"Once again," Tenn's thumbs tapped quickly on the screen. "I'll tell her you're overwhelmed by grief, but you think you can survive another day here."

"This is so cool," Sumo said.

Casey said to Noah, "We'll get all this stuff done and then we'll go riding."

"Awesome!" Noah's face fell. "What about Billy da Pug?"

"No sweat. Dylan is going to ride in Tenn's camping backpack." Casey shrugged out of his backpack. "Billy da Pug is little. He can ride in mine."

"Great!"

Tenn wasn't so sure. "Won't Billy da Pug hop out?"

"Nah." Noah scratched the top of the pup's head. "We'll bring the stick."

"Okay then." Tenn went back to his cell phone and his thumbs got busy on the screen. "Megan is working in Roxy's stall. She's in charge while I'm gone. Tell her when you finish grooming Nell. I want Megan to start training her today. Harry, you're coming with me."

Harry waved a hand around the stable. "There's a million things to do."

"Later. We can discuss the plans for the sports ranch on the way to the hospital." Tenn put his cell phone in his pocket and smiled. "I've got a good feeling about today. When Toby starts remembering, we'll find out who hurt him and why."

Harry nodded. "I'll meet you out front."

SIXTEEN

Noah leaned the stepladder against Nell's stall. "Done!" He dropped to the ground, brought his knees up to his chest and put his head down. "Thanks for helping. Empire is so tall I could've gotten a nosebleed brushing his mane."

Sumo sank down beside him. "It was a good idea for us to groom the horses together. Makes it go faster."

"Move over." Casey tossed Sumo and Noah bottles of water before sitting crossed legged beside them. He pulled his backpack onto his lap and got out Dylan's collapsible water dish. "Over here, Little Buddy." Casey patted the ground. When Dylan came over, he poured water into his dish. "Drink up."

You bet. Watching you work is thirsty business.

Casey showed Noah the water dish, but Noah shook his head and pointed to Billy da Pug. The pup was passed out next to his stick. His mouth was partially open, and the tip of his pink tongue was poking out.

Sumo drained his water bottle. "Let's groom Nell next."

Nell was watching them but kept cropping at the hay in her bucket.

"What was with her and Harry?" Noah ran a hand over his head. "Does she really hate his bald head?"

"I was just messing with Dad." Sumo got to his feet and dusted dirt from his shorts. "She was probably still stressed out from the trip."

Noah leaned back against the railing. "She seems to be better now."

"Dylan calms her down." Casey pulled Dylan close to him.

Dylan stretched his muzzle across Casey's lap. *Nell knows I'm her friend.*

Casey ran a hand down Dylan's back. "We'll groom her. Right, Little Buddy?"

Dylan bounced to his paws and his stubby tail tick-tocked left and right. *Yes!*

"We got this." Casey stood up. "But stick around just in case."

Sumo pulled out his cell phone and sent Noah a look. "Sure."

"Sit where Nell can see you," Casey said to Dylan. "Then she won't be nervous."

Okay. Dylan followed Casey into Nell's stall.

Casey took Nell's lead rope and tied her to the railing. "Easy girl." Casey ran his hand down her nose. "We'll go slow."

It's going to be all right. Dylan sat in front of Nell. *You can trust Casey.*

"Lights. Action. Video," Sumo boomed.

Dylan spun around. *What, what and what happened to your voice?*

"Geez Sumo," Casey hissed over his shoulder. "Why are you talking like that?"

"Howdy, Dylan's Dog Squad fans." Sumo held his cell

phone high, and his face filled its screen. "We come to you live from Tenn Hundred Acres Ranch in Lake Arrowhead, California. Say hello to Dylan and his friend Nell, a one-year-old filly." Sumo showed Nell to the viewers and brought his cell phone down to Dylan.

Arf!

Sumo turned the screen on himself again. "Welcome to Horse Grooming 101. Today

Casey will groom Nell. As you know Casey trains dogs at Dream Big K-9 Academy in Brea, California, and wants to have a dog training school of his own. Maybe someday he'll train horses, too." Sumo turned his cell phone around to Casey. "What do you have to say to our fans?"

Casey tossed a handful of hay in Sumo's face.

Sumo huffed out a breath and shook his head, sending the hay flying. "Loyal Dylan's

Dog Squad fans, watch and you'll learn how to groom a horse."

Dylan watched.

Noah watched.

Nell watched.

Dylan's Dog Squad fans watched.

"Fine," Casey muttered and took a deep breath. "First, make sure your horse can't get away from you."

Sumo's cell phone scanned the stall, showing where Nell was tied to the railing with a lead rope.

"Make sure your horse sees you." Casey stepped in front of Nell. "Some horses will bite so you want to say hi, like this." Casey used the back of his hand to nose bump Nell very gently. "Your horse will learn to nose bump you back."

Nell nose-bumped Casey back.

"Hey, she did it." Noah clapped twice.

Good girl. Dylan's chest puffed out with pride. *You're so smart.* Dylan studied his paws. *I wish I had hands.* Dylan sighed. *I wish I could clap.*

"Important. Never stand behind your horse. You might get kicked." Casey slowly ran a right hand over Nell's chest as he walked to her left side. "Grooming makes your horse look good and your horse will learn your touch is good. If your horse shies away during grooming, check her out. Maybe your horse has hurt itself."

Sumo balanced on one foot and shoved the grooming bucket toward Casey with his other foot. The video screen jumped and caught the roof of the stable.

"This," Casey pulled out a plastic oval and held it up, "is a curry brush. It has teeth on it." Keeping his left hand on Nell's side, he rubbed in circles with his right hand. "Work the curry brush like this to bring up dirt. Use good pressure but don't use the curry brush on the horse's face or inside the legs. It's too hard. Horses are really sensitive there."

Casey tossed the curry brush into the bucket and pulled out another brush. "This is a dandy brush. Use it to brush away the dirt on the horse. Kind of like a broom but don't brush too hard." He ran the brush over his bare arm and flinched. "It can hurt."

Casey held onto the dandy brush, and rooted around in the bucket until he found another brush. "This is a body brush and looks just like a dandy brush." Casey held both up and waited until Sumo got closer. "It's important to know the difference. You can use the body brush on your horse's face." Casey started at the top of Nell's head and carefully brought the brush down her nose. "Use it anywhere your horse is sensitive. Like on the inside of its legs."

"What's that silver thing?" Sumo pointed to the bucket.

"This," Casey picked up a silver curved hook, "is a hook pick. At least once a day clean all the manure, rocks, and gunky stuff from your horse's hooves. If you don't the hooves can get infected." Casey kept his right hand on Nell's side and moved to her back legs.

Dylan shook out his dusty front paws. *Casey shampoos my paws.*

Nell shifted her weight.

"Ho Nell." Casey waited a moment. "Stand next to your horse. Remember, don't stand behind your horse." Casey gave Nell a gentle pat on her rump before slowly letting his left hand glide down her leg and pick up her hoof.

Sumo stepped in and crouched, bringing his cell phone within inches of Nell's hoof. "You're seeing it first, Dylan's Dog Squad fans!"

"Back up, Sumo," Casey warned and tapped Nell's shoe with the tip of the hook pick. "Find this spot on the horse's shoe."

Casey has shoes. Nell has shoes. Dylan looked down at his front paws. *Not me.*

Casey put the hook pick in and pulled toward him. Manure flew out splattering Sumo and his cell phone.

"Sorry!" Casey grinned.

"Yeah, right," Noah cracked up. His own cell phone was out and video rolling. "Look over here, Sumo. Man, you're a mess."

Sumo scowled and wiped the gunk away. "You did that on purpose." He backed up.

"The mane and tail are last." Casey stood up and brushed his palms off. "Start with a detangler but don't soak the mane." Casey lifted sections of Nell's mane and gave it a light mist. Then he hooked the spray bottle to his shorts and ran his fingers through Nell's mane. "Use your fingers to undo the knots before you use the mane and tail brush." He got a knot out. "When you brush, get a small section of the horse's mane, start at the bottom and work your way up." Casey picked up a section of Nell's mane and brushed. "If you start at the top, you'll tear out the horse's mane and it will hurt." He moved his hand a little higher up the mane and brushed some more.

Nell rubbed her cheek against Casey's arm.

She likes it!

"Good girl." Casey patted her cheek. "It's the same idea for the tail." Casey kept his right hand on Nell's side and walked back. "Never."

"Stand behind the horse," Noah called out.

"Exactly." Casey stood off to Nell's side and sprayed her tail with the detangler. "Horses like to swish their tails, causing knots and tangles. Use your fingers to take them out." Casey worked two knots free. "The tailbone is here." He wrapped his hand around the tail about one-quarter of the way down. "Start brushing at the end of the tail, one section at a time, and work your way up and past the tailbone."

Nell cast a look over her shoulder at Casey and whinnied.

Don't worry. Casey grooms me all the time. Dylan sidled over so Nell could see him better. *You're doing great.*

"Just like the mane, if you start brushing from the top down, the hair will break off and you'll hurt your horse."

Dylan shook out his ears. *Casey brushes my ears, starting at the bottom.*

"Summer means fly weather." Casey reached into the bucket for another spray bottle. "When you're done, spray your horse lightly with fly spray. If your horse is really bothered by flies, it can wear a fly mask to protect its eyes." Casey shrugged. "That's it."

Nell leaned against Casey and blew air through her nose.

"You catch on fast." Casey pulled a molasses and alfalfa treat out of his pocket and gave it to her. "Good girl."

Nell backed up, spread her hind legs, kept her left front leg straight, knelt with her right leg and lowered her head.

Wow!

"Nell!" Casey gasped. "That's awesome!"

"Cut!" Sumo announced. "That's a wrap!"

Cut what? Wrap what?

Casey hugged Nell. "You can bow."

"Check this out." Noah was studying his cell phone. "You're getting hits already."

"I bet the video goes viral." Sumo beamed.

Casey held out another treat to Nell. "You earned it."

Nell agreed and swallowed it whole.

"Amazing!" a voice sang from the shadows.

Casey jumped and put a hand over his heart. "Megan!"

"Sorry. I didn't mean to scare you. That was quite the show." Megan gave them a hearty hand clap and the palomino with her tossed up its head.

Panic flashed across Casey's face. "We were, uh. You, uh, should've said something."

"And get in the way of your big movie making moment?" Megan laughed. "Oh no."

"Busted," Noah said out of the corner of his mouth.

"We were, uh, we'd been working," Sumo stammered, "but uh, we were just taking a break." He grabbed Noah by the arm. "This is Noah. Our friend. The video was his idea. He was helping us."

Dylan whined. *I was helping too.*

"What?" Noah squeaked. "Uh, I'm only here because Tenn was supposed to take me to practice but my coach got sick."

"Relax." She gave them an easy smile. "Webster and I enjoyed it. Especially the bow."

At the mention of his name Webster tipped his head and swished his tail.

Megan reached up and rubbed his cheek. "Yes, you can bow too." Webster used his nose to flick Megan's braid over her shoulder. She laughed. "Now you're showing off."

Casey changed the subject. "Tenn said you'll start training Nell today."

"Yes. Because Harry is at the hospital, I'm also training the new ranch hands. The trouble is Webster would really like to go for a ride," Megan let out a sigh, "but I don't have time."

Webster flattened his ears and put his head down.

"I know, I know." Megan scratched him under his chin. "You're not happy about it."

Webster bumped his big head against Megan's arm, snorted and then rested his head heavily on her shoulder.

"I'm getting to the good part, okay?" she said and patted Webster's nose. "So, guys, I'm in charge while Tenn is gone. He gave me a list of your chores, but the new ranch hands can manage them. Would you do me a favor and take Webster, Rocket, and Empire for a ride?"

Sumo stepped closer. "You mean it?"

"You bet!" Noah's happy smile faded. "Wait. Does that mean I have to ride Empire? He's gotta be the tallest horse on earth."

"Big deal." Sumo grinned. "He almost never bucks anybody off."

"It only hurts when you hit the ground." Casey laughed. "Be sure to roll away from his hooves."

Noah grimaced. "Thanks."

"Don't listen to them. Empire is really a big baby." Megan ran a hand over Webster's mane and kissed his nose. "Be a good boy." She handed Webster's lead rope to Casey and reached for Nell's. "Trade you."

"Okay."

Megan stroked Nell's nose. "Where are you going riding?"

"Uh," Casey waved his hand in the air, "around. You know."

"Noah's never been on the ranch," Sumo added.

Noah shook his head left and right. "Never."

Megan arched one eyebrow and waited.

Sumo, Casey, and Noah smiled.

Whine.

She gave up. "Okay then. Mrs. Hudson wants you back in time for lunch."

Dylan's stomach growled. *We should have lunch first.*

Megan pointed to each of them. "No one rides without a helmet, got it?"

"Sure," they promised.

I don't have a helmet.

When Megan was out of sight they huddled together.

"What's the plan?" Sumo asked.

Casey didn't hesitate. "We're going after Fernando."

"That's it?" Sumo frowned.

Oh, brother.

SEVENTEEN

"We need these." Casey tossed water bottles, Dylan's collapsible water dish, Dylan's leash, and the treat bag out of his backpack.

I need a treat. Dylan picked up the treat bag with his front teeth. *Now.*

Casey started filling the pockets of Tenn's backpack with their stuff. "We have everything."

Dylan waggled the treat bag in front of Casey. *I don't have my treat.*

"Okay." Casey looked around the stable. "That's it."

Hardly. Dylan heaved a sigh and plunked his rump down. *Please don't make me beg.*

"What, Little Buddy?"

Dylan tossed his head and the treat bag landed at Casey's feet. *Arf!*

"Sorry." Casey broke a peanut butter cookie in half and gave it to Dylan. He popped the other half into his mouth, chewed and made a face. "Not as good as Mom's."

Whine.

"You're right. We won't tell Mrs. Hudson. We don't

want to hurt her feelings." Casey got out Dylan's collapsible water dish and filled it. "She tried."

Thanks. Dylan drank and then licked his lips. *I feel better now about the whole thing.*

Sumo, Noah, and Billy da Pug came over.

"How much longer?" Casey asked.

"I need to get Billy da Pug ready." Noah held out his hand. "Give me your backpack."

Casey tossed it to Noah. "There are towels in the tack room next to the helmets. You can use some for a cushion."

Dylan pawed Casey's leg. *Do I get a helmet?*

"Sounds good." Noah asked, "What's the rest of the plan?"

"Everybody's working so the bunkhouse will be empty. We'll ride over and go through Fernando's stuff to prove he's the bad guy."

"That's your plan?" Sumo put both hands on his hips. "That's dumb."

Dylan whined. *The plan could use some work.*

"We need Fernando's right glove," Noah reminded Sumo, "to prove he's the bad guy."

"What if we don't find it?" Sumo's voice went up a notch. "What if we get caught?"

Sumo is making some excellent points.

"There's no way we're going to get caught," Casey reasoned. "The ranch hands are working. We'll be in and out in a heartbeat. This plan will work one hundred percent. It's so simple it's guaranteed to work."

I don't think guaranteed means what you think it means. Whine.

"How?" Sumo demanded. "What if."

"Look," Casey talked over him, "since we have Fernando's left glove that means we've already done fifty percent of the plan. Finding his right glove is all we need. That's the other fifty percent. Fifty plus fifty means we'll have one hundred percent success."

Dylan sighed. *More like having one hundred percent chance of getting caught.*

"This isn't just dumb," Sumo said through clenched teeth. "This is stupid."

Whine.

Casey checked the time. "We need to saddle up." He stood and handed Webster's lead rope to Noah. "We'll take Empire. Dylan likes to be up high."

Dylan whimpered. *No, I don't.*

Noah smiled. "Thanks."

Dylan hunkered down and watched Casey, Sumo and Noah haul towels, helmets, saddle pads, saddles, and halters out of the tack room. *That's a lot of stuff.* Dylan counted three helmets. *What? No helmet for me?* He put his muzzle on his paws and heaved out a sigh. *So disappointed.*

"We have to be back by lunchtime." Sumo grabbed his gear and headed to Rocket's stall. "Hurry."

"No problem." Noah took a saddle pad and got to work on Webster.

"Saddling a horse is pretty easy," Casey said to Dylan. He put the saddle pad on Empire and smoothed it out. "It's better to cross the stirrups and cinches—these leather straps, over the top of the saddle and around the horn before putting it on the horse." Casey did and then hefted the saddle on top of Empire. He pulled the stirrups and cinches down. "I've ridden Empire before, so I know which notches to use."

Dylan watched Casey pull long straps down and put them through metal rings, before pulling the long straps up and through more rings. *This is a lot of work for one horse.*

Being a dog is better. One collar, one leash and I'm good to go.

"Easy boy." Casey gently bent Empire's front two legs at the knees to stretch out his belly. He slipped his hand under the leather strap. "If the horse's skin gets caught under the cinch it hurts." He patted Empire. "Just right."

Whew.

"The halter is next." Casey picked up something with thin leather straps and buckles and walked in front of Empire.

This is a lot to remember.

"Horses don't see the way we do," Casey explained. "Your horse always needs to know where you are." Casey stroked Empire's neck, then placed the halter over his nose and guided it up to his cheekbone. "The crown piece goes on top of the horse's head." Casey slipped it behind Empire's ears.

Empire's ears are on top of his head. Dylan wagged his head. *My ears are on either side of my head. I can't wear a halter.*

"There." Casey buckled the halter.

Empire blew air through his nostrils.

"We'll meet you out front," Casey called to Sumo and Noah. He put his helmet on, took Empire's reins, grabbed some towels and Tenn's backpack. "C'mon, Little Buddy. Time to get you in the backpack."

Dylan raced out of the old stable and over to the bike rack. *Time to ride!*

"You're going to love riding." Casey dumped everything on the ground before tying Empire to the bike rack. "You can smell and see all kinds of stuff."

I want to see everything.

Casey got Tenn's backpack out of Dylan's trailer and

held it up. "It's big but that's okay." Casey folded four towels, stuffed them inside, and stood the backpack on end. He compared the backpack to Dylan. "We need more towels."

I'm just a little guy.

Casey added two more towels and then the cushion. "Want to try it out?"

Dylan danced on his hind legs and pawed the air. *Pick me up!*

"Okay." Casey got Dylan under his front legs and slowly lowered him into the backpack. "Are you sitting on your cushion?"

Arf! Dylan tried to rest his muzzle on the opening of the backpack. *I can't see.*

Casey rolled the top of the backpack down until it was below Dylan's shoulders. "That's better." He brought Dylan's front legs out and put them on the rolled down part. "When I put the backpack on, lean forward and put your paws on my shoulders. Then you won't flop around when we ride."

Okay.

"Here we go." Casey shrugged into the backpack and fastened the strap in front. "What do you think?"

Dylan leaned forward. *Arf!*

"Ow!" Casey clapped a hand over his ear. "No barking, okay?"

Sorry. Dylan licked Casey's ear.

Casey untied Empire. He gripped the saddle horn, put one foot in the stirrup, swung his leg up, and lost his grip.

Dylan's head snapped back. *Agh!*

"Holy, moly, joly." Casey caught the saddle horn before he landed on his butt. "I didn't think about this part."

Think about it now!

Casey brushed his hair out of his eyes and looked around. "Over here." He led Empire to a bench and climbed on it. "We're lucky Sumo wasn't here. He'd be laughing about this for a week."

Yup.

"Okay. Here goes." Casey put his foot in the stirrup. "Horses spook easily." He held onto the saddle horn and struggled to heft himself up. "I have to swing my leg high and over Empire's flank. If my leg hits Empire, he'll take off."

Swing your leg really high. Dylan looked over the side of the backpack. *The ground is a long way down.*

Casey made it and settled in the saddle. "How are you doing?"

Dylan put his paws on Casey's shoulders. *Let's go.*

"Sumo and Noah are coming."

Sumo and Rocket trotted over. "Ready?"

"Waiting on you."

Dylan gave Sumo a tongue-hanging-out-of-his-mouth grin. *Empire is a cool ride.*

"Oh yeah?" Sumo held up his cell phone. Casey, Dylan, and Empire filled the screen. "This is my favorite part of the video. You nearly ate it!"

Sumo's right.

"Sumo!" Casey swiped at the cell phone and missed.

Sumo busted up. "I just posted it. No one has seen it."

"Sorry to take so long." Noah came alongside them and pulled up on Webster's reins. "I was watching the video." He laughed. "Dylan's Dog Squad fans think you should stick to grooming horses."

Casey glared at Sumo.

We should take Sumo's cell phone away from him.

"Thanks again for the backpack. Billy da Pug is liking

it." Noah reached back and patted the pup's little black and tan head. Billy da Pug's two black eyes were peeking out of the backpack and his stick was beside him. "Where are we going?"

"We'll cut across the field, so the horses will get a good run." Sumo leaned forward in his saddle and pointed to a pile of rocks. "There's a path through the woods. We'll go slow so the horses can cool off. The bunkhouse is on the other side."

We finally get to ride. Dylan rested his muzzle on Casey's shoulder and sighed happily.

Casey tapped Empire with his heels and the big horse tore off.

Dylan's head jerked back. *Hey!* Dylan leaned forward and his muzzle banged up and down on Casey's shoulder. *Agh!* Dylan's ears flapped up and down in the wind. *Oh!* Dylan's paws scrabbled for a hold on Casey's shoulders. *Can't!* His buns thumped, thumped, thumped on his cushion. *Help!* Dylan snuggled closer to Casey and closed his eyes. *When does the fun start?*

Minutes later Dylan felt Empire slow, and he opened his eyes. Dylan saw the woods and relaxed. *At last.*

Sumo called back over his shoulder, "The path is narrow. We have to go single file."

Noah went after Sumo and Casey followed. In the woods shadows washed over them and the air was cool. Birds screeched past, flying low. A squirrel scampered up a tree and watched them from a branch.

Dylan lifted his head and scented the air. *The woods is a busy place. Lots of smells.* A cool breeze blew over his face. *Nice.*

When they broke through the woods Sumo urged Rocket into a trot. Casey and Noah picked up the pace and followed Sumo to a two-story bunkhouse with a wide porch. A long railing and horse trough ran the length of the porch.

Sumo tucked his helmet under his arm, got off Rocket and looped the reins around the railing in a double slip knot. "Water your horses here."

"The bunkhouse looks deserted." Noah used both hands to shield his eyes from the bright sunlight.

"Told you." Casey hooked his helmet over the saddle horn, slid off Empire and tied him up. Empire immediately stuck his face into the trough and began to drink. "Hold on Dylan." Casey wrestled his way out of the backpack, stood it on end and lifted Dylan out. "Did you like your first ride?"

My buns are numb. Dylan shook himself out. He cast his eyes upward. *My topknot is sticking out all over.*

Casey cracked up. "You look like Einstein."

Not funny. Who's Einstein? Dylan kicked out his front legs and then tried kicking out his back legs. *My back legs are bent forever.* Dylan body bumped Casey. *I like riding in my car seat better.*

Noah clipped Billy da Pug's leash to his collar and walked him over. "Which room is Fernando's?"

Sumo made a face. "Dunno."

"We'll find it." Casey shrugged. "How hard can it be?"

Sumo was having second thoughts. "What if we don't find Fernando's glove? What if he took it with him?"

"No way." Now Casey made a face. "Who wears only one glove on a ranch?"

Who thinks this is a good idea?

They climbed the three steps to the porch. Casey put his finger to his lips, signing Quiet to Dylan. Noah did the same to Billy da Pug.

"I bet the bunkhouse is locked." Sumo brightened. "We should leave."

Casey brushed past him and tried the door. It opened without a sound, and they crept inside.

It's really quiet in here. Kind of creepy.

Bedrooms lined both hallways. They looked inside the first four bedrooms. Each one had one bed, one footlocker, one dresser, one desk and chair, a braided area rug and one TV. One bedroom had clothes scattered about but the others were neat.

"There's gotta be like twenty bedrooms in this place," Noah said. "We could be here all day."

"Told you this was a dumb idea." Sumo turned around. "Let's go home. I'm hungry."

Me, too. Dylan's stomach growled. *Listen to Sumo.*

"Wait." Casey grabbed Sumo's arm. "I've got an idea."

Sumo jerked his arm away. "No more dumb ideas."

Casey pulled Fernando's glove from his cargo shorts pocket and knelt beside Dylan. "This is Fernando. Dylan, find Fernando."

"Can Dylan do that?" Noah asked.

"Dylan has a great nose." Casey let Dylan sniff the glove. "He can find anyone or anything."

Dylan wrinkled his snout. *Fernando doesn't smell very good.* Dylan sat down. *Sumo's right. Let's go home.*

Casey gave Dylan the scent again. "This is Fernando. Dylan, find Fernando." Casey smoothed Dylan's topknot down. "The sooner you do this, the sooner we can get lunch."

Okay. Okay.

Dylan put his nose to the ground, going from bedroom door to bedroom door. At the end of the hall, he went to the staircase. He sniffed along the first stair, put his front paws on it and turned back to Casey. *Fernando was here. Whine.*

Billy da Pug strained on his leash. *Heh, heh, heh.*

Noah signed Quiet to Billy da Pug and shortened his leash. "Does Dylan have something?"

Casey gave Dylan the scent again. "This is Fernando. Dylan, find Fernando."

Dylan trotted up the stairs. In the hallway he put his nose to the ground and walked in figure eights. Then Dylan headed to the first bedroom on the right. He went inside, sniffed around, came back, sat, and alerted. *Arf!*

"Good boy." Casey ruffled Dylan's ears. "Start looking guys."

Hooray. Then it's time for lunch. Dylan followed Casey inside, sprawled across the braided area rug, and rubbed his muzzle over the rough surface. *I hope Mrs. Hudson makes grilled cheese sandwiches.*

"Not much here." Sumo opened and shut the dresser drawers. "A few T-shirts. Some bandanas. No glove."

"The guy travels light." Noah closed the closet door. "An old jeans jacket. That's it."

Casey ran his hands under the pillow on the bed and held up a cell phone. "This is interesting." He frowned. "Oh man. It's locked."

Sumo took the cell phone from him. "Gimme Fernando's glove."

Casey handed it over. "Now what?"

"Criminals use gloves, so they don't leave fingerprints at the scene but that's how they get caught." Sumo turned the leather glove inside out. "They're too dumb to know they always leave fingerprints inside the glove."

"My mom told me that," Noah said. "But I've never seen it done."

Sumo tried pressing the thumb of the glove to the cell phone. "Yes!"

"Oh wow! It worked." Casey grinned and punched Sumo on the arm. "Watching all those dumb crime shows finally paid off."

Good job Sumo!

"They're not dumb." Sumo scowled at Casey but scrolled through recent calls. "Fernando called the same number four times yesterday." Sumo took his cell phone out of his pocket, found an app, tapped in the phone number, and looked up. "Tompkins Ranch."

Noah leaned over his shoulder. "How do you know?"

"Got Your Number app." Sumo grinned and slid his cell phone into his shorts pocket. "Gotta love the internet."

"That proves," Noah got excited, "Fernando is working for Mr. Tompkins."

Dylan cocked his head and his ears pricked. A rumble started low in his chest. *Grr.*

"What, Little Buddy?"

Dylan sprang to his paws and the rumble in his chest exploded into sharp barks. *Arf! Arf!*

Fernando stood in the doorway. A coil of rope hung from one shoulder. Rage burned his cheeks but the hand pointing the gun on them was steady. "We meet again."

EIGHTEEN

Billy da Pug yipped and scurried behind Noah. *Heh, heh, heh.*

"Stay." Casey held Dylan back by the shoulders.

Let me at him. Dylan danced in place. *Arf! Arf! Grr.*

Fernando slid cold eyes Dylan's way. "Shut your mutt up or I will."

I'm not a mutt. I'm an American Cocker Spaniel. Dylan wrestled away from Casey and sprang.

Casey caught Dylan and held him tight. "Not now, Dylan."

When? Dylan snarled and double pawed the air.

"Dylan? That's a big name for a fluffy dog." Fernando laughed. "He looks like a pair of Ugg boots."

I've got forty-two teeth, Buster. You won't be laughing when I bite you. Dylan wiggled and Casey put him on the ground. *What are Ugg boots?*

"Stop, Little Buddy."

Why? He started it.

"You're talking different. When we met," Sumo stepped

closer, "you used small words and had an accent. I thought English was your second language."

"Don't believe everything you hear, kid." Another laugh. "I grew up in Malibu. I have a master's in business administration from USC."

Sumo, Casey, and Noah exchanged looks.

"What's going on?" Sumo demanded. "Why are you working for that scumbag Tompkins? Why did you hurt Toby?" Sumo zeroed in on the rope Fernando was carrying and his voice stuttered. "Uh, why do you have rope with you?"

"Let's just say," Fernando smirked, "I was inspired when I saw you come in here."

"Why are you doing this?" Casey asked.

"What is this, twenty questions?" Fernando waved the gun toward Noah. "Ask your friend here. I warned him the other night in the woods." He frowned. "This is your fault. You should've listened and backed off."

"I'm deaf," Noah signed and said.

Fernando gave a disgusted grunt but didn't lower the gun. "Don't that beat all." He glanced around him. "I'd love to stay and chat, but the clock is ticking. Here's how this is going to go." He shrugged off the coil of rope and let it drop. "You," he kicked the rope over to Casey, "the one with the mouthy mutt. Tie up your friends' hands and feet."

"You'll never get away with this," Sumo protested.

"Get serious," Fernando scoffed and went to the dresser. He pulled bandanas from the middle drawer and threw them on the bed. "Gag them. Tie the black and tan dog's leash around that kid's wrist. I don't want the dog running off."

Casey stayed where he was.

"Now!" Fernando ordered and tossed Casey his multitool folding knife. "Cut the rope with this. Don't get any bright ideas or your fluff dog buys it."

Dylan looked from Fernando to Casey. *What am I buying?*

Casey did as he was told. "You only had two bandanas. Now what?"

"No problem." Fernando pointed to the desk chair. "Sit down and put your hands behind your back."

"What about Dylan?"

"Shut up."

Casey sat. "Hey," he complained when Fernando tied his hands and feet, "that's really tight."

Dylan bared his teeth. *Don't hurt Casey!*

"That's the idea." Fernando checked the knot. "Get your dog over here so I can muzzle him."

"No."

"Maybe," Fernando mused, "I'll take him with me. I bet dogfighters would pay a lot of dough for a cute dog."

"Come here, Little Buddy," Casey coaxed. "It's okay."

Dylan belly crawled to Casey and stretched out at his feet. *I'll never leave you.*

Fernando cut a length of rope. Quickly he looped it around Dylan's snout, tied it around his ears and behind his head. "That should do it."

Dylan pawed at the rope and rolled to his side. *It's hurting my ears.*

"So you don't feel left out." Fernando gave Casey a tightlipped smile and cut a longer length of rope. "Open wide." He placed the rope between Casey's teeth. "Now you and your mutt match."

Grr. I'm not a mutt!

Fernando shoved his multitool folding knife into his

jeans pocket, gave them a mock salute and left. A few seconds later they heard the front door bang shut.

Casey bumped his chair hard against the desk, but it stayed on the ground. He tried rocking side-to-side, but the chair didn't tip. Casey raised his legs up and tried a scissor kick. He screamed in pain through the rope gag, dropped his feet to the ground and shook his head.

Dylan stretched his fluffy paws out in front of him. *I wish I had hands. Then I could untie you.*

Sumo and Noah were kicking out with their feet and making a racket, but the ropes stayed around their ankles. Casey tried rocking the chair again.

I have to help. Dylan front pawed at the rope. His toenail snagged it and the rope tightened around his muzzle. *Ow!* He flipped onto his back and tried bringing his back paws up to scratch at the rope. *Nope. My legs are too short.*

Casey, Sumo, and Noah stopped what they were doing and watched.

I can't let them down. Dylan gave it all he had and rolled. The rope around his muzzle slipped a little. *A little can become a lot.* Dylan rolled and rolled and rolled, working himself across the braided rug.

There's got to be an easier way. Dylan got to his paws and gave a full body wag. The rope slipped off his muzzle and pooled at his paws. Dylan gave Casey a toothy grin. *How about that!*

Casey, Sumo, and Noah started making happy sounds through their gags.

Billy da Pug joined in. *Heh, heh, heh.*

Hold on. Dylan sidled up to Casey, then worked his muzzle into Casey's shorts pocket and snuffled around inside. *Yes!* His snout got hung up inside the pocket. *No! I can't breathe.* Dylan yanked his muzzle free.

Casey hip boosted himself to his side and mumbled through the gag, "Get my knife."

I'm trying. Dylan worked his nose into the pocket again. His teeth clamped around Casey's Swiss Army knife. *Got it!*

Muffled cheers came from Sumo and Noah.

Heh, heh, heh.

Dylan dropped the knife into Casey's lap. *Arf!*

Sumo and Noah did a butt bounce up and down and their feet stomped the floor.

Yay! Dylan spun around in a circle but stopped when he saw Casey hadn't moved. *Oh yeah. Your hands are still tied behind your back.*

Casey slumped in the chair and groaned.

I'm sorry. Sadness hit Dylan hard, and he hung his head. *I tried my best.* Dylan felt his sad turn to mad. *I should've bitten Fernando when I had the chance.* He thought about that, and hope bubbled inside him. *I don't have hands, but I have forty-two very sharp teeth.* Dylan trotted around Casey and gave the knot a closer look. *That's a big knot. I have to get it loose.* He sank two incisors into the knot and munched. *Tastes awful!* Dylan munched until his jaws ached. *I won't give up. I've got to try harder.* Angling his head, he hooked his upper and lower canines into the knot and tugged.

Nothing.

Dylan tugged again and the knot relaxed.

Yippee!

Dylan went back to work, nibbling and tugging, again and again. The rope suddenly gave way. Dylan flew back and landed on his rump. *Ow!* Dylan wobbled to his feet and went around to Casey. *Well?*

Casey untied his gag and ruffled Dylan's ears. "Getting my knife was a great idea," Casey pulled Dylan into a hug, "but using your teeth got me free. You're so smart."

Dylan leaned against Casey. *We're the best team.*

Sumo and Noah went back to kicking the floor and bouncing on their buns.

"Oh yeah." Casey cut the rope from his ankles and then set to work on theirs. "Sorry guys."

"Thanks." Sumo worked his jaw left and right. "I thought we'd be stuck here forever."

"What now?" Noah rubbed feeling back into his ankles and wrists. "Go get Fernando?"

Dylan pawed Casey's leg. *Go get lunch.*

"Something's been bothering me," Casey said and put his knife away. "It's weird Fernando showing up like that. How'd he know we'd be here?"

Sirens shrilled from somewhere and came closer.

Oh no.

Casey, Dylan, and Sumo ran to the window.

"What's going on," Noah asked and hurried over.

Two cruisers pulled in front of the bunkhouse. Sirens bleeped again and then cut short. Deputies hopped out of the cruisers. Some got into position, taking cover behind their doors. Others held guns out and sprinted for the porch.

"I don't believe this," Sumo wailed.

Dylan put his front paws on the windowsill and smooshed his snout against the window screen. *They look really mad.*

"That's Sheriff Ridley." Noah groaned and closed his eyes. "My mom's boss."

The big man confirmed it by holding up a radio and

announcing, "This is Sheriff Burton Ridley. Come out with your hands up. I'm not asking you twice."

"We gotta get outta here." Casey spun away from the window. "We'll take the horses and cut through the woods. The path is too narrow for their cruisers."

Noah shook his head. "Are you nuts? We can't outrun the deputies!"

"We've got to try," Casey argued. "We can't get arrested again. We're still on probation."

Me, too.

"This is your fault." Sumo fisted both hands in his hair. "I told you this was a stupid idea." He jabbed Casey in the chest. "I'm never going to get into Harvard. I'll never be anybody. I'll never make the cover of *Fortune* 500. I'll spend the rest of my life eating gruel in some overcrowded prison with no air conditioning, watching reruns of Jeopardy, and wearing an orange jumpsuit with cheap tennis shoes and no socks."

"What's Sumo talking about?" Noah grabbed Casey's arm. "You're on probation?"

"Well, yeah," Casey peeled Noah's hands off, "but it wasn't our fault."

Yes, it was.

Sumo threw up both hands. "Our friends from Dream Big K-9 Academy borrowed a ton of money from The Sledgehammer, a notorious crook and loan shark, and they couldn't pay it back, so Casey had a lamebrain idea to break into The Sledgehammer's house and steal the loan papers, but the cops showed up and we got arrested and hauled off to jail and then we were put on probation."

Me, too. It was so embarrassing.

"Oh wow." Noah thought about that. "That took a lot of guts. You're good friends."

Oh boy.

"Thanks." Casey scooped Dylan up and held him close. "Get Billy da Pug. We gotta move."

"What if we told the truth?" Sumo brightened and then frowned. "Or is Sheriff Burton the kind of guy who shoots first and asks questions later?"

Noah picked Billy da Pug up. "He hardly ever shoots anybody."

What about little dogs?

"What's the truth?" Casey argued. "We didn't find Fernando's glove. We have no proof of anything."

They headed for the door but didn't make it. Two deputies holding guns appeared and blocked the doorway.

"Stay where you are," the female deputy ordered. "Show us your hands."

Dylan sat up straight in Casey's arms and raised both paws. *I remember this part.*

"Oh hi," Sumo began weakly. "I'm Sumo Modragon. This is my dad's ranch. Can we help you?"

"You heard Deputy Lansky," a male deputy with a thick neck and a head the size of a bowling ball bellowed. "You're under arrest."

Deputy Lansky turned away and spoke into her radio. "Three males in custody and two dogs." She paused. "What kind of dogs?" Her eyes skimmed over Billy da Pug and landed on Dylan. "Short. Requesting backup."

"You got this all wrong," Sumo protested. "We're the victims here."

The second deputy snorted and pulled out his cuffs. "That's what they all say, kid."

NINETEEN

Sumo checked his cell phone. "We've been sitting here one hundred and twenty-seven minutes. What's taking Sheriff Ridley so long?"

I'm bored and I'm hungry. Dylan uncurled himself, got to his feet and stretched. *This floor is hard.* Dylan hopped onto the wooden chair next to Casey. *Not comfy.* He did a full circle on the seat, plopped down and wiggled his buns. *I need my bike cushion.* Dylan rolled onto his side, kicked out with his back paws, and slid off the chair. *Oh!*

Casey slouched in his seat and stretched his long legs out in front of him. "It could be worse."

Dylan shook himself out and hooked his front paws over Casey's thigh. *Pick me up.*

"Are you insane?" Sumo grumbled. "We're in Sheriff Ridley's office. We've been arrested for burglary—again. Our next stop is the slammer."

Sumo is making some excellent points. Dylan leaned forward. He hitched up a back paw and hopped on one foot, trying for Casey's lap. *Agh!* Dylan slid back down. *Your lap is too high.*

"We haven't actually been arrested," Noah corrected him. "We're just not free to go."

Dylan sat and ran his nails down Casey's bare leg. *I don't want to go to the slammer.*

"Sorry, Little Buddy." Casey picked Dylan up and settled him on his lap. "I bet Sheriff Ridley is trying to find Tenn. When he does Tenn will tell him who we are and why it was okay for us to be at the bunkhouse."

Sumo chewed on his lower lip. "I called Dad, but he doesn't pick up."

"He can't." Casey glanced his way. "Hospitals have rules about using cell phones."

"That's right." Sumo got happy. "I bet Sheriff Ridley went to the hospital to get him."

"Maybe," Noah leaned back in his chair, "but none of this other stuff makes sense. Who called and reported a burglary?"

Fernando.

Sumo, Casey, and Noah thought about that for half a second. "Fernando."

Told you.

"What if," Casey shifted Dylan on his lap and faced Sumo and Noah, "Fernando saw us go inside the bunkhouse. He was afraid we'd find proof he's the bad guy, the one who attacked Toby. He called the tip into the Sheriff to stop us."

"There was nothing in his room," Sumo reminded him. "Not even his glove."

"He must've hidden the proof in the bunkhouse." Noah shook his head. "We missed it."

Dylan's stomach growled. *We missed lunch.*

"I'm starving," Sumo toed Casey's backpack with his sneaker. "Got anything to eat?"

"Mrs. Hudson made peanut butter cookies." Casey took a cookie out of the treat bag and passed the rest to Noah and Sumo. "They're not as good as Mom's," Casey gave half a cookie to Dylan, "but they're okay."

Sumo bit in and chewed. "Kind of dry. Ms. D's cookies are better."

"You're lucky your mom bakes." Noah broke off a piece for Billy da Pug and ate the rest. "Homeless people wouldn't eat my mom's cookies."

Thirsty. Dylan raised his muzzle up to Casey and coughed once. *Hint, hint.*

"Okay." Casey found a bottle of water in the backpack. He filled Dylan's collapsible water dish before handing the bottle to Noah. "Here."

"Thanks." Noah waited until Billy da Pug ate his cookie to show him the water. Billy da Pug ignored him and begged for more cookie. Noah brushed off both hands before using his first two fingers to tap them against his thumb, signing No.

Arf! Billy da Pug disagreed. *Arf! Arf!*

Billy da Pug barked!

"I never heard him bark." Sumo laughed. "He must really like peanut butter cookies."

"Mostly," Noah showed Billy da Pug his empty hands, "he likes food."

Billy da Pug huffed and snuffled Noah's hand.

"Waiting sucks." Sumo tipped back in his chair and put his feet on the Sheriff's desk in front of him. He brought out his cell phone again. "What's the address here? Want to order a pizza?"

Yes! I want cheese pizza. It's my favorite. Whine.

"Before Sheriff Ridley comes in, we need to get our

story straight," Casey said. "He's going to ask why we were in the bunkhouse."

"Okay," Noah agreed. "What should we say?"

The office door opened.

"Mom!" Casey jumped up.

Mom! Dylan slid off Casey's lap and hit the floor. *Hey!*

She didn't smile. "Get your feet off Sheriff Ridley's desk, Sterling Modragon."

Sumo's feet crashed to the floor, and he sat up straight. "Yes, Ms. D."

"Busted!" Noah grinned.

"Excuse me, Colleen." Liz Melodia slipped past her and stood in front of Noah. She was wearing jeans and a cotton shirt. When she put her hands on her hips, her shirt rode up, showing her gun. "Noah."

"Uh, hi Mom," Noah mumbled. He reached down for Billy da Pug but wasn't fast enough. Billy da Pug scurried under Noah's chair, peeked out and put his face on his paws. His little black eyes fixed on Liz and didn't blink.

Dylan searched Mom's face. *Are we in trouble?*

"Casey," Mom kept her voice even, "I just drove two hours in rush hour traffic. Start talking."

We're definitely in trouble.

"Hey, this is like so great." Casey went from surprised to chipper. "We've missed you. Right, Little Buddy?"

Dylan whined. *You're on your own.*

"Boys," Liz cut in. "Sheriff Ridley is holding you on a burglary charge. What's that all about?"

"Burglary?" Casey echoed and looked puzzled. "No idea." He jerked a thumb toward Sumo. "We were showing Noah around the ranch. You know because he'd never been there before."

"Yeah," Sumo chimed in. "We stopped by the

bunkhouse because it has a water trough for the horses, and we'd been riding the horses and the horses were tired."

"That's right," Noah added. "The horses were really tired and thirsty."

Mom got them back on track. "Why were you upstairs?"

"Upstairs?" Casey's eyebrows dipped together. "We were downstairs, and the bedroom doors were open. Noah saw inside and wanted to know if all the ranch hands had the same stuff in their rooms." Casey smiled sweetly. "You always say showing is better than telling so we took him upstairs. We stopped at the first bedroom for a look."

"Noah?" Liz signed and asked.

Noah signed and said, "Casey and Sumo were right. All the bedrooms are the same."

Whine.

"Uh," Casey changed the subject, "why did Sheriff Ridley come out to the ranch?"

Liz angled her head. "Dispatch received an anonymous tip. The caller said three suspicious males entered the bunkhouse. After what happened to Toby, Sheriff Ridley decided to check it out."

"Who is Toby?" Mom interrupted. "What are you talking about?"

"Let's start from the beginning." Liz began with Ronny's arrest in San Bernardino and ended with Toby's accident. "Tenn is at the hospital. Toby is conscious but he doesn't remember anything." Her mouth set in a grim line. "We found nothing at the crime scene and cleared it late last night. I'm afraid we're no closer to finding out who did this than when we started."

"Boys." Mom's eyes traveled from Casey to Sumo and landed on Dylan. "When were you going to tell me about this?"

Don't look at me. I'm a dog.

"Mom! You were working." Casey gave a half laugh.

Mom didn't.

"We were waiting until we knew something, Ms. D. We didn't want you to worry."

Mom and Liz both frowned and folded their arms across their chests.

"Mom mafia," Casey and Sumo said under their breaths.

We're done for. Whine.

There was a quick knock and Sheriff Ridley stepped in. "Detective Melodia, Ms. Donovan." He nodded to them before taking a seat behind his desk. "Thank you for coming." He got to the point. "Sorry about holding the boys but after what happened to Toby, we had to check the tip out."

"Why would someone see three boys at the bunkhouse and think they had anything to do with Toby's accident? That's quite the leap of imagination. Besides," Mom reasoned, "everyone on the ranch knows Sumo and would know he had a right to be there."

"Until we investigated, we had no way of knowing the call was a prank. If the caller is discovered," Sheriff Ridley gave a quick nod of his head, "he'll answer to me and be charged with Penal Code 148.3, Making a False Report of an Emergency."

Big deal. Put Fernando in the slammer.

"When we arrived, the boys were in the upstairs bedroom and a coil of rope was on the ground along with a lot of cut rope." Sheriff Ridley opened his iPad and referred to his notes. "I talked to Harry Biggs. That's Tenn Stillwater's foreman. Harry said the room belonged to Fernando Huertas."

"Hold on." Casey held up a hand. "What do you mean belonged?"

"Harry said Huertas had been waiting on a job. It came through and he left this morning."

"What about his stuff?" Sumo leaned forward in his chair. "We saw a jeans jacket in the closet."

Sheriff Ridley shrugged. "The guy was in a hurry."

No kidding. He was in a hurry to rat us out.

"Casey was right about Fernando," Noah whispered to Sumo.

Mom went on Mom Alert. "You knew the room was Fernando's?"

Uh-oh. Mom is so smart.

"How could we?" Casey gave her a wide-eyed look. "We've never been in the bunkhouse before."

"Mm-hmm."

Mom switched to Dylan.

Me, neither. Whine.

"Now what Sheriff?" Liz asked.

"The boys are free to go. Tenn and the ranch hands are donating blood for Toby at the hospital. He asked if Ms. Donovan could take the boys back to the ranch."

"No problem." Mom smiled. "I'm staying at the ranch tonight."

"Wait," Casey squeaked.

Mom raised one eyebrow. "What happened to the part where you missed me?"

"Uh, I mean wait until you see Tenn's new basketball court," Casey managed a quick save. "It's really cool."

"Does Dad know you're staying?" Sumo asked.

"Tenn said I was invited anytime." Mom took her keys from her purse. "Remember?"

"What about the horses?" Noah tapped Casey on the arm. "We left them at the bunkhouse."

"They're fine," Sheriff Ridley assured him. "I had Megan pick up the horses and take them to the stable. She also took your bikes back to the house."

"Thank you, Sheriff." Mom stood up and checked the time. "I'll call Mrs. Hudson and tell her we'll be a little late for lunch."

Casey, Sumo, and Noah high-fived.

Yay! I'm starving.

Liz broke up the merry moment. "Not so fast. You have things to do at home."

"But we haven't had lunch," Noah argued.

Dylan's stomach rumbled. *I'm really starving.*

"I'll make you something at home," Liz said.

"I'd rather eat dirt," Noah muttered.

Liz's dark eyes snapped to his. "What?"

"I'd rather eat *dinner*," Noah said loudly, "at home. Mrs. Hudson promised us lunch."

Liz was firm. "Next time.

Mom turned to Sheriff Ridley. "What happens to Toby's case now?"

"We've run out of leads." He gave a palms up. "Looks like the case is closed."

That's what you think. Dylan sat up straight. *Dylan's Dog Squad is on this.*

TWENTY

Mom parked in front of Tenn's house next to a canary yellow Corvette convertible. "That's some car."

"It's Mrs. Hudson's," Sumo said. "She has a cool ride."

"She does indeed." Mom nodded toward their bikes. "It was nice of Megan to deliver your bikes. Be sure to put them away."

"Yeah, Mom."

"Thanks for getting us Chub Bub's Subs, Ms. D. They were great."

I love roast beef subs. They're my favorite. Dylan licked his lips. *I love veggie and cheese subs, too.* Dylan sighed happily. *All subs are my favorite.*

"You're welcome. Sorry we were too late for lunch at the ranch," Mom turned in her seat, "but Mrs. Hudson is barbecuing ribs for dinner."

Really? Dylan looked down at himself. *Casey tickles my ribs.*

"What's for dessert, Ms. D?"

"That's the best part." Mom's eyes lit up. "Carrot cake with homemade vanilla ice cream."

I love carrot cake and I love vanilla ice cream! Dylan shoulder-bumped Casey. *They're my favorites.*

"Awesome." Casey unbuckled Dylan's seatbelt.

"I have to run an errand, but I'll be back in time for dinner." Mom handed Casey a bag. "This is for Dylan."

For me? Dylan's heart sighed. *You're the best mom.*

Casey opened the bag. "Shampoo and conditioner. Why?"

Dylan whined. *Why do I have to get wet all over?*

"You really have to ask?" Mom gestured to Dylan's fur caked with dirt and twigs. "He's filthy."

Aw Mom. Dylan hung his head. *That's not a very nice thing to say. Whine.*

"Carry him inside and straight up to the bath. If he gets dirt on Mrs. Hudson's floor, you won't get any barbecue." She gave them The Look. "You should've been more careful."

Hey! It's not my fault I got dirty. I was trying to catch a bad guy. Dylan licked Casey's cheek. *Carry me. I want to eat.*

"Do a good job washing Dylan and don't make a mess."

"Yeah, yeah." Casey shoved the shampoo bag into his backpack and helped Dylan out of the car.

"Bye, Ms. D." Sumo got out and they watched her drive away. "A lot happened today. It feels like we left the ranch a hundred years ago."

"I know." Casey laughed. "Meanwhile back at the ranch."

Dylan slid a look to Casey. *Huh?*

"Of course, we're back at the ranch." Sumo stared at Casey. "What's so funny?"

"I've always wanted to say that." Casey stared back at

Sumo. "C'mon. You never heard anyone say 'Meanwhile back at the ranch' before?"

Nope.

"Nuh-uh."

"Sumo! In every Western movie somebody always says, 'Meanwhile back at the ranch' when they go back to the ranch." Casey cracked up. "That's funny."

No, it's not. Dylan leaned against Casey. *Maybe 'Meanwhile back at the ranch' doesn't mean what you think it means.*

Sumo smirked. "Get serious."

"Forget it."

"If you have to explain a joke," Sumo insisted, "it's not funny."

Sumo's right. It's not funny.

"I said forget it." Casey glared at him.

"Don't get sore." Sumo went up the front steps and ran his sneakers through the boot scraper. "Want to watch a movie before dinner?"

"Yeah. What?"

"A Western."

Not funny.

"Knock it off." Casey took the front steps two at a time and dumped his backpack at the front door. "Mom was right, Little Buddy." He held up Dylan's front paws. "They're really dirty." Casey ran his sneakers through the boot scraper twice. "Too bad you can't use this."

Too bad I can't wear sneakers.

"Hold on." Sumo slowly opened the front door, poked his head inside and then whispered over his shoulder. "The coast is clear."

"The coast is clear," Casey snorted. "That's dumb. We're not on the beach."

Casey is making an excellent point.

"Get inside," Sumo hissed, "before Mrs. Hudson sees us."

"Okay. That makes sense."

"Boys." Mrs. Hudson stood in the middle of the foyer.

"Mrs. Hudson!" Sumo clapped a hand over his heart.

"That's it. I'm asking Tenn." Casey looked all around. "There's got to be cameras somewhere."

"She freaks me out." Sumo muttered under his breath. "She's always watching."

"That's my job, Sterling." Mrs. Hudson's pudgy hand pointed to the stairs. "Use the blue towels in the upstairs guest bathroom for Dylan. Don't put them in the hamper. Bring them down to the laundry room when you're finished."

"Got it," Casey promised and hugged Dylan. "Thanks." Her voice warmed. "We want Dylan to look spiffy."

Thank you, Mrs. Hudson.

"I was on my way out." She came closer and patted her black patent leather shoulder purse. "This is my afternoon off."

Dylan leaned forward and saw his reflection in her shiny purse. *There's a smudge on my muzzle. I've got twigs and dirt in my topknot and my legs are covered in gunk. Mom was right. I'm filthy.*

"The ranch is really quiet," Sumo said. "Where is everybody?"

"Harry was at the hospital. He stopped by and said Toby is beginning to remember. The doctors are running more tests. After that the deputies will talk to him. Harry said he was going to the old stable to check on Nell and to make sure Megan worked with the other horses today."

"Where's Harry now?" Casey asked.

Mrs. Hudson shrugged. "Probably went back to the hospital. The ranch hands are still donating blood."

"That's good news about Toby." Sumo gave a thumbs up.

Mrs. Hudson started to go. "More good news is Sheriff Ridley questioned Jedd Nightwalker and he admitted to hitting Tenn's Jeep with his truck. He's been cited."

"Great," Casey agreed.

They followed her out and waited while she got into her car.

"Wave goodbye, Little Buddy." Casey lifted Dylan's paw and helped him wave.

"Mrs. Hudson's going, going," Sumo stood on tiptoes and watched until her car disappeared, "and she's gone. We're free." He grinned happily. "She's like having a senior citizen mom."

"Mrs. Hudson's not so bad. She's nice to Dylan." Casey put Dylan down. "Let's go to the backyard."

"What about Dylan's bath?"

"You heard Mrs. Hudson. Everyone's gone. We got plenty of time."

Yippee! Dylan scampered ahead. *No bath.*

"This way, Dylan." Casey headed toward a striped chaise lounge.

"Today turned out okay." Sumo dropped into another chaise, stretched out and pillowed his head on his hands. "We didn't get arrested, and Fernando's gone. It's over."

"We only know Fernando is gone." Casey put Dylan on the chaise lounge and wiggled in beside him. "We don't know why any of this happened."

"Amazing. You can ruin anything."

"This isn't over." Casey held up his thumb. "Ronny

tried to steal Nell." Casey's index and third fingers went up. "Fernando attacked Toby and Noah."

"So it doesn't make sense, big deal. Fernando is gone."

Whine.

"Why did Fernando go to all that trouble," Casey tapped his fourth finger, "to scare us at the bunkhouse? He was leaving anyway."

"Dunno. Don't care." Sumo closed his eyes. "Let it go."

"But."

"Stop. Talking." Sumo's cell phone pinged. He sat up and took it out of his pocket. "Noah says he's stuck cleaning his room." Sumo's thumbs got busy. "I'm telling him we're having barbecued ribs for dinner. Mrs. Hudson always makes a ton of food. Ask Ms. D if he can come."

"Nap first." Casey leaned back and toed off his sneakers. "I'm beat."

"Me, too." Sumo gave a huge yawn. "It's really quiet out here."

"Yeah. I like it." Casey shut his eyes and wiggled his toes.

Dylan studied his furry paws. *I wish I could wiggle my toes.* Dylan stretched his muzzle across Casey's lap. His nose quivered. *No toes but I've got a great nose.* He raised his head and scented the air. *Something.* Dylan scented the air again and caught a whiff. *Smoke.* He pulled himself upright and slapped a paw on Casey's stomach. *Smoke! Arf!*

"I'm trying to sleep." Casey lazily scratched the top of Dylan's head. "Not now."

Now! Dylan pounced on Casey's chest, knocking the air out of him.

"Dylan!"

Arf! Dylan brought his muzzle close to Casey's face. *Arf! Arf!*

"Quiet, Dylan," Sumo mumbled but opened one eye. "Holy, moly, joly!"

"What?"

"Get up!" Sumo jumped to his feet and shook Casey's arm. "F-fire!"

Casey bolted upright and Dylan tumbled to the ground. "Sorry, Little Buddy." Casey jammed his feet into his sneakers and helped Dylan to his paws. "Where?"

"There!" Sumo pointed to wisps of brown smoke spiraling upward in the blue summer sky. "The old stable." He fumbled in his pocket for his cell phone. "I gotta call Dad."

Casey was quicker. "9-1-1," he said into his cell phone. "This is Casey Donovan at Tenn Hundred Acres Ranch. The old stable is on fire. Send help." Casey listened. "No one is here." He tossed up his free hand. "I don't know *why not*." Casey rolled his eyes and repeated, "Send help."

"Are they coming?" Sumo stammered. "What do we do now?"

Hurry, guys. Dylan was already running and leading the way. *The horses are in trouble!*

"Get our bikes," Casey raced behind Dylan, "and get over there. Do what we can."

"Like what?" Sumo huffed behind him, his short legs trying to keep up with Casey's long ones.

A gust of wind blew the smell of smoke their way. *Uh-oh.* Dylan searched the sky. *The smoke is getting stronger.*

They rounded the corner of the house and sprinted to their bikes. Sumo angled into his bike helmet and swung his leg over his bike. Casey slapped his helmet on, knelt in front of Dylan's bike trailer and unzipped its front screen.

Nell is in trouble. Dylan jumped inside and circled once on his cushion. *Zip up the screen. We got to roll.*

"Hang on and lie low. Try not to breathe in the smoke." Casey pushed off and they bumped along the dirt road to the old stable.

Dylan pressed against the side screen anyway and tried to see. Smoke and dust blew in and he pawed at his eyes. *Smoke stings my eyes and hurts my throat. It's hard to breathe.* He hunkered down on his cushion and sucked in air. *Better.* Dylan kept low until he felt the bike skid to a stop. *We made it.* Fire engine sirens sounded in the distance. *Hurry!*

Casey unzipped Dylan's screen on the bike trailer. "Only the hay loft is on fire. If the old stable catches on fire, it won't take long to burn."

Dylan stepped out and watched fire race up the walls of the hay loft. *Oh no.*

Sumo hopped off his bike and tossed his helmet on the ground. "What now?"

A hay bale toppled from the hay loft, hit the ground in front of Dylan and broke apart. *Yip!* Dylan jumped back.

"Dylan!" Casey grabbed him up and hugged him tight.

Fingers of fire greedily snatched at the hay, leaving nothing behind but black marks on the ground. *Hay burns fast.*

You're squishing me. Dylan kicked out with his back paws. *Put me down.*

"Okay but no wandering around." Casey put Dylan down, pointed his finger and said sharply, "Stay."

It's rude to point your finger. Dylan plunked his butt on the ground but turned his face away. *Sign language is more polite.*

The fire engine sirens sounded louder.

"They won't get here in time." Sumo whirled around. "We got to save the horses!"

"Only Nell is inside. Mrs. Hudson said Megan was exercising the other horses."

"We don't know that for sure!" Sumo put both hands on his hips and stepped up to Casey. "Quit arguing!"

Yeah, Casey. Quit arguing. Dylan strained to hear horse sounds but there was only the sound of fire. *Nell must be so scared.* Dylan watched the flames shoot into the air. *I'm scared.*

"It's crazy to go in." Casey blocked Sumo when he made a move for the old stable. "We need to wait for the fire department."

Dylan pawed at Casey's leg. *We need to get moving.*

"Are you going to help me or not?" Sumo fisted his hands, but his lower lip trembled.

"We can't do anything," Casey insisted.

Not if you just stand there! Dylan whined and ran to the door. *I can try.*

TWENTY-ONE

Dylan ran hard. When he went inside the old stable a blast of heat hit him in the face. *Yikes!* He slowed and gave a quick look around. *No fire down here, only brown smoke. That's good.* Dylan started running down the passageway, glancing at stalls as he went. *Empty.* He kept going. *They're all empty. Mrs. Hudson was right. The horses are safe.* Dylan blew out a happy sigh and shook his topknot out of his eyes. *I'm coming Nell!*

Dylan picked up the pace and didn't stop until he reached Nell's stall. *Empty. Very strange.* He stood at the open gate and scented the air. *Nell was here.* Dylan padded over to the grooming box and put his nose inside. *These are Nell's brushes.* He snuffled around and the dandy brush fell out of the box. *She needs a lot of brushes to look great.* He used his teeth to drop the brush inside. *I have only one brush and I always look great.* Dylan looked down at the dirt and hay caked on his blond fur. *Well, except for now.* Putting his nose to the ground he sniffed, going from corner to corner of the stall. *Where's Nell?*

Dylan raised his snout and scented the air. *Megan was*

here. He zigzagged back and forth across Nell's stable, keeping his nose to the ground. *Hmm. Somebody else was here.* He tried again. *Somebody familiar.* Under a clump of hay Dylan spotted something lumpy and brown. He pawed at the hay and found a leather glove with a ragged cuff. Dylan's nose quivered lightly over the glove. *I know this smell. This glove belongs to Fernando. He took Nell!* Dylan picked up the glove with his teeth. *I'll bring it to Casey. He'll know what to do.*

Above Dylan the wood ceiling snapped and crackled. *Time to move.* He looked carefully around him and thought fast. *I came in through the front door and down the passageway. I'll go back that way.*

Crash!

Dylan raised his head to the sound and saw flames peeking through the rafters. *Uh-oh.* He inhaled and caught the scent. *Fire!*

Wood beams rained down in the corner of the stall, bringing a whoosh of smoke and dust. Dylan's eyes watered and he coughed once, dropping the glove. *It's getting scary in here.* He shook out his muzzle, spraying Fernando's glove with dog spit. *I need Casey.*

"Dylan!"

Dylan tried an arf, but his bark got lost in the sounds of the fire. He swallowed and tried a bigger bark. *Arf! Arf, Arf!*

Dylan saw Casey and Sumo coming through the smoke. *Yes!* He gathered his paws under him and leaped, knocking Casey down. Dylan planted his paws on Casey's shoulders and covered his face with sloppy dog kisses.

"You scared me." Casey gently pushed Dylan off. "All of a sudden, you were gone."

"You just took off," Sumo griped. "You needed to wait for us."

I needed to save Nell. Dylan flicked his ears and looked away. *You were too busy arguing.*

"The hay loft caught the stable roof on fire and that's bad. The good news is the fire department just got here. We ran inside before they could see us and tell us not to go in." Casey grabbed Dylan in a hug. "I'm glad you're safe."

I'm glad you came. Dylan muzzle-rubbed Casey's cheek. *We're a team.*

Casey glanced around. "Where's Nell?"

Exactly. Dylan brought Fernando's glove over to Casey, dropped it in front of him and slapped a paw on top of it. *Whine.*

"Look." Casey turned the glove inside out and showed Sumo the initials. "FH."

"I knew it! This proves Fernando is the bad guy." Sumo crowed. "We got to tell Sheriff Ridley."

Casey ran a hand over Dylan's ears. "Good job, Dylan!"

Dylan leaned into the rub. *It was nothing.*

A crash came from the entrance. Outside, boots pounded the ground, and voices shouted, "Get the hoses!"

Around them the old stable let out a massive groan and shook. Thunderous sounds of water hitting the old stable were followed by the smell of smoldering, wet wood.

Uh, guys.

"The hay loft must've fallen in." Sumo whirled around to Casey. "That means the front door is blocked."

That means there's no way out.

Casey coughed and waved the smoke away from his face. "The old stable is next."

Fear hit Dylan's chest like a fist. *We're trapped!*

"Great. Just great," Sumo moaned. "Now what?"

Casey huffed out a breath. "Help me find something of Nell's."

"What? Later!" Sumo grabbed two fistfuls of Casey's T-shirt and hauled him to his feet. "We need to get out!"

Listen to Sumo.

"We need something of Nell's," Casey pried Sumo's hands off, "so we can give Dylan the scent."

"Are you nuts? The old stable is on fire!"

Sumo is making some excellent points.

"Fernando took Nell," Casey said calmly. "If Dylan can find Nell, we'll find Fernando."

"Really?" Sumo hesitated. "Are you sure?"

Casey laughed. "You should know. You're the one who watches all those dumb crime shows."

"Hey!" Sumo punched him in the arm.

Guys! Dylan swung his muzzle from Sumo to Casey. *We're on fire, remember?*

Casey cast a look around the stall. "There's got to be something."

We got to go. Dylan stood on his hind legs and planted both paws on Casey's thigh. *Now.*

Sumo tossed up his hands. "Like what?"

Like this. Dylan went to Nell's grooming box, pulled out the dandy brush and brought it to Casey. *Here.*

"You're so smart. Ready to catch a bad guy?"

Ready to get out of here.

Sumo turned to Casey. "Do you have a plan?"

"Of course."

Not.

"Oh yeah?" Sumo grabbed Casey's arm. "What?"

Casey shrugged. "We'll figure it out as we go."

Figures.

In the passageway Casey brought the dandy brush close to Dylan's nose. "This is Nell. Dylan, find Nell."

Got it. Dylan walked in figure eights up and down the

passageway. *Nell didn't go out the front door.* Dylan stopped. *The familiar person smell is with her. The same familiar person smell from Nell's stall.* He put his nose to the ground again. *Arf! Follow me.*

"The tack room is that way," Sumo argued. "Is Dylan sure?"

Of course. I'm a dog. Dylan plunked his rump down and alerted. *Arf!*

"Dylan's got a great nose. He's sure."

Thanks, Casey. Dylan swiped a paw across his eye. *It's really getting smoky in here. Time to go.*

Sumo wasn't convinced. "Why the tack room?"

"It's got a back door and it faces the woods." Casey tossed up both hands. "Don't you get it? Fernando set the fire in the hay loft because it's above the front door."

"Right!" Sumo got excited. "Fernando knew the fire department would be too busy putting out the fire and wouldn't see him take Nell through the woods."

It's getting hard to see in here. Dylan panted. *And really hot. Can we go now?*

"If we hurry, we can catch up." Casey gave Dylan the scent again. "This is Nell. Dylan, find Nell."

Dylan kept his nose to the ground and his butt in the air. When he got to the back door of the tack room he leaped up and hit the safety bar with his front paws. The old wooden door swung open, and Dylan charged outside. Casey and Sumo were right behind him.

"Hey, you!" a firefighter in yellow and black fire gear shouted. "What were you doing in there?"

"Uh, uh," Sumo stammered.

"I'm Casey Donovan. I called 9-1-1." Casey grabbed Sumo's T-shirt and dragged him close. "This is Sumo Modragon. Tenn Hundred Acres is his dad's ranch."

"Oh yeah?" The firefighter zeroed in on Dylan.

Casey picked Dylan up. "This is Dylan."

Whine.

The firefighter wasn't impressed. "Answer me. What were you doing?"

"We were checking the stable for horses." Casey waved behind him. "They're gone."

Chatter came from the firefighter's radio. Keeping his eyes on them he said, "The back is clear except for two kids and a dog." The firefighter listened to more chatter from the radio. "What kind of dog?" he repeated into the radio and ran his eyes over Dylan.

Dylan sat up straighter. *American Cocker Spaniel.*

The firefighter's eyebrows dipped into one long line. "Short."

Geez.

"You're busy out front," Casey said cheerfully and put Dylan down, "so we'll go through the woods."

"Make it snappy." He spoke into his radio again. "Going in to clear the stables." He clicked off, gave them a stern look, then strode away.

Casey waited until the door closed before giving Dylan the dandy brush. "This is Nell. Dylan, find Nell."

Dylan put his snout to the ground. *Arf!* He trotted to a narrow dirt road running through the woods. He stopped and sniffed at the first tree. *Nell and the familiar person were here. Arf!*

"Nell is too young to ride. Fernando will have to walk her through the woods, so they'll be going slow." Casey tried to see through the trees. "Isn't this a shortcut to Highway 189?"

"Yeah." Sumo pushed a branch aside. "So?"

"The woods is the perfect place to hide a horse trailer.

Fernando only has to get Nell to the trailer, then onto Highway 189 and they're both gone for good."

We got to get to Nell first. Dylan raced through the woods ahead of Casey and Sumo. When the road curved Dylan saw blue sky peeking through the pine trees. *Almost there.* The sun's rays glinted off something shiny. *Horse trailer?* Dylan ran faster and tripped over a tree root. *That hurt.* He got to his paws and looked down. *A bandana.* Dylan sniffed at it. *It doesn't belong to Megan or Fernando.* He tried again. *It has the familiar person smell on it.* He looked back and saw Casey and Sumo coming around the curve.

Casey called, "Keep going!"

Sumo was red-faced and puffing hard, but he sent Dylan a wave.

Hurry up, guys. Dylan picked up the bandana and took off. At the edge of the trees, he spotted a truck hitched to a horse trailer. *I was right!*

Snorts came from the trailer, followed by rapid kicks and the trailer rocked.

Nell! Dylan padded to the passenger's side of the trailer and crouched low. *I see two legs and two cowboy boots on the other side.* Hot air blew Dylan's ears away from his face. *The truck's engine is on.* Dylan hauled his head back trying to look into the cab of the truck. *I can't see. The firefighter was right. I'm short.*

Casey and Sumo broke through the trees and ran over to Dylan. Dylan jerked his muzzle up and flung the bandana at Casey.

Casey caught it one-handed. "Did you find this in the woods?"

Arf!

"I bet Fernando dropped it," Sumo said.

Not Fernando. Whine.

"Yeah." Casey stuffed it into his shorts pocket.

Sharp kicks rocked the trailer again.

I know you're scared Nell, but we'll save you.

"Nell's freaking out. Help me get her out of there." Sumo started for the trailer.

The truck's engine revved.

"There's no time. Fernando's getting away." Casey searched the empty field. "Call Noah."

"Why?" Sumo had his cell phone out, but his hand was shaking.

"Tell him to call Sheriff Ridley. Hurry!"

Sumo's fingers danced over the screen. "Where are you going?"

"To the driver's side. We have to stop him." Casey tapped Dylan on his shoulder and put his index finger to his lips, signing Quiet.

Forget quiet! We need to save Nell. Run! Dylan took off with Casey close behind him. When they came around the horse trailer, they saw Fernando reach for the truck's door.

"Stay back, Dylan." Casey looked over his shoulder and spotted Sumo with his cell phone out and video rolling. "Is help coming?"

A siren's wail answered the question.

"Oh yeah." Sumo bobbed his head up and down but kept glued to his cell phone screen. "This is so awesome. I bet Dylan's Dog Squad gets a zillion hits."

"Not now Sumo."

Not now Sumo. We have to save Nell.

"Out," Fernando yanked open the door, reached inside and tossed Harry out of the cab. Harry landed flat on his back, but his fists were up.

Whoa!

"You're crazy," Harry shouted. "I'm gonna call the cops."

"Go ahead." Fernando leaped on top of him, and they started slugging it out in the dirt.

Dylan raced toward them, then circled Fernando and Harry. When they rolled past him, Dylan caught Harry's scent. *You're the familiar person. The bandana is yours. You took Nell.* Dylan jumped between Harry and Fernando. *Grr!*

"Dylan! No!" Casey yelled. "Get down."

Dylan ducked. Harry landed a right hook to Fernando's jaw. Fernando's hand flew to his jaw, and he glared at Dylan. "Thanks a bunch."

Oops! Sorry about that. Dylan clamped down hard on Harry's wrist. *Grr! Grr!*

"Let go of me!" Harry screamed.

Dylan shook his wrist hard. *You're the bad guy.* Dylan shook harder. *You were stealing Nell!*

Harry slapped Dylan across the face with his free hand. "You stupid mutt!"

Ow! Dylan saw stars but didn't let go. *I'm not a stupid mutt. I'm an American Cocker Spaniel. You're stupid for stealing Nell. Arf!*

Harry flung his arm wide, sending Dylan flying. "This will teach you."

Yip! Dylan landed on his side and struggled to catch his breath.

Fernando stepped over Dylan, spun Harry around and decked him. Harry hit the dirt and stayed there. "Now we're even." Fernando hefted him to his feet. "It's over."

"Dylan!" Casey raced to Dylan and crouched beside him. Very gently Casey raised his head. "Little Buddy."

TWENTY-TWO

Dylan let out a long, low whine. *That hurt.*

Casey jumped to his feet. He pushed Fernando aside and gave Harry a hard two-handed shove to the chest. "You hurt Dylan!"

Dylan wobbled to his paws. *Let me at him.*

"Dylan attacked me. I didn't mean to hurt him. I, I was defending myself." Harry tried a sad smile and hung his head. "I'm so sorry."

This is my smile. Dylan drew his lips back and bared his teeth. *You're not sorry. You're just sorry you got caught.*

"You're lying." Casey clenched his fists and got in Harry's face. "I saw you."

Sumo came closer and held up his cell phone. "I got it on video."

You're the bad guy. Dylan snapped at the air between them. *Not Fernando.*

"This isn't what it looks like. I caught him stealing Nell. He attacked me," Harry pleaded. "You got to believe me."

No, we don't. Grr! Grr!

Fernando sliced his hand through the air. "Save it."

Sweat broke out on Harry's forehead. He reached into his back pocket but came up empty. He ran a shaky hand over his head instead. "You can't prove I had anything to do with this."

Arf! Arf! Dylan got on his hind legs and gave Casey's pocket a nose bump. *We can prove it.*

"Looking for this?" Casey took the bandana out of his pocket and held it up. "Dylan found it on the trail in the woods. You dropped it when you were stealing Nell."

That's right.

"It's a bandana, so what?" Harry's upper lip curled but he kept his eyes on the bandana.

"Your smell is on it." Casey waved the bandana under Harry's nose. "Your smell and Nell's smell are on the trail too. That proves you stole Nell and brought her here."

Harry batted the bandana away. "Ha!"

The siren sounded louder. Harry's eyes cut to the road, and he licked his lips. Fernando, Casey, Sumo, and Dylan boxed him in.

"Harry Biggs," Fernando flashed his badge, "you're under arrest."

"You're a cop?" Casey blinked. "No kidding."

Dylan stopped mid-grr and shook out his ears. *No kidding.*

Sumo's eyebrows shot up. "That's so cool."

"Yup. I'm the good guy." Fernando shoved his badge back into his pocket. "Here's my favorite part." He turned Harry around, pulled a pair of handcuffs from his waistband and slapped them on Harry's wrists.

Dylan gave Fernando a forty-two teeth canine grin. *Make the handcuffs really tight.*

"We had nothing." Fernando nodded once at Dylan. "Thanks to you, we're going to close this case today."

Casey and Sumo helped. We're Dylan's Dog Squad.

"Way cool." Sumo's eyes got big. "So, is this case about some slick international horse smuggling operation that's been ripping off horse owners and then selling the horses on the black market?"

Fernando's mouth twitched but he kept his smile to himself. "Harry is part of Tompkins' horse smuggling team. They steal expensive horses from ranches and then sell them to private buyers."

"Oh man! You're going down, down, down!" Sumo pumped his fist into the air. "You'll never see the light of day again."

Fernando looked from Sumo to Casey.

"Sumo watches too much TV," Casey said.

Fernando let that go. "Nell was a birthday present from Manuel Ramirez to his ten-year old daughter, Angelina. Tompkins stole Nell from the Ramirez Horse Ranch in Mexico. The kid's been crying her eyes out ever since."

That's sad.

"Oh yeah." Sumo had his head down and was working the cell phone screen again. "I read about that. Nell's real name is Canela. It means cinnamon in Spanish." He looked up. "Makes sense. Nell, uh Canela, is a reddish-brown horse."

She'll always be Nell to me.

Sumo went back to the screen. "They're offering a big fat reward." He grinned at them. "I wonder if it's in pesos or dollars."

"Not now Sumo." Casey held his left hand, palm upward and brought his right hand down to his left hand at a right angle, signing Stop.

Stop, Sumo.

Fernando went on. "A buyer paid Tompkins a big bag of

money for Canela. Tompkins was supposed to deliver her this week."

"But," Casey jumped in, "Tompkins lost her in a blackjack game to Tenn."

Bummer.

"Yup," Fernando agreed. "The buyer was Augie Cipriano, a really bad guy who doesn't like mistakes. Tompkins was desperate to get Canela back before Cipriano found out."

Uh-oh.

"If Cipriano found out Tompkins lost Canela," Casey guessed, "Cipriano would make him pay, big time."

"Oh yeah. People who cross Cipriano tend not to live very long. So, Tompkins sent Ronny to steal her, but you know what happened there." Fernando smirked. "Serves him right. Ronny rolled over on Tompkins before the deputies got him to the station." He barked out a laugh. "Never hire cheap labor. The guy was dumb, but he was smart enough to cut a deal."

"Wow," Casey and Sumo said.

"We knew Tompkins had an inside man on Tenn Hundred Acres Ranch. We didn't know who, so I went undercover to find out."

A black, shiny Chevy Suburban with flashing lights shot off Highway 189 and bounced across the field, sending up clouds of dust. The SUV stopped on a dime and its siren gave one final blast.

"Looks like the gang is all here," Fernando announced.

Sumo aimed his cell phone at two men and one woman in ugly polyester suits and sensible shoes getting out of the Chevy Suburban. "Who would wear a suit to a horse ranch?"

"FBI?" Casey glanced at Fernando. "You, too?"

"Like I said, I'm the good guy."

"I don't get it. If you're the good guy, why did you grab Noah in the woods?" Sumo turned his cell phone to Fernando.

"Not now," Casey warned.

Not now. Sigh.

Fernando brushed the cell phone aside. "I didn't. I was chasing Harry in the woods and would've caught him, but Noah got in the way. I was *warning* Noah about Harry, but I had no idea he was deaf. Noah got scared and took off. Then you two came along." He gave a disgusted snort. "You nearly blew my investigation." He gave another snort. "You wouldn't back off. The next thing I knew you were tossing my room at the bunkhouse. Geez. I couldn't get rid of you."

"Sorry," Casey and Sumo mumbled.

You could've said something. Whine.

"It's hot out here," Harry complained. "I want a lawyer. I want to cut a deal. I can give you names."

"You'll get your chance," Fernando promised.

"Before you get thrown in the slammer," Sumo moved in front of Harry, "why did you attack Toby?"

"He got in the way."

"Why set the hay loft on fire? You worked at Tenn Hundred Acres a long time," Sumo said quietly. "Dad trusted you and paid you a lot of money."

Harry smirked. "Tompkins paid me more."

I'm a dog and even I know that's a confession.

"That's so low." Casey picked up Dylan and held him close. "Toby could've died. The horses could've died."

"No way," Harry retorted. "I made sure the horses were gone before I started the fire." He rolled back his shoulders. "I wouldn't hurt a horse."

"A criminal with priorities," Sumo muttered.

The FBI agents split up. The two men went to the horse trailer. The woman in aviator glasses and a blue suit strode over and nodded to them. "Hi Brandon. We came as soon as we got your call. Sheriff Ridley's on his way, too." She glanced around. "Looks like you got things handled here. Nice job."

"Leslie Vanders," Fernando tipped his head, "meet Casey, Sumo, and Dylan. They get the credit."

"Brandon?" Casey and Sumo cracked up.

"His real name is Brandon Ashworth." Leslie grinned. "Did he mention he's from Malibu?"

"Shut up," Brandon said dryly.

Leslie took off her aviator sunglasses and smiled at Dylan. "Hello, handsome." She brushed his topknot out of his eyes and leaned closer. "You have the longest eyelashes I've ever seen. I'm jealous!"

You think I'm handsome? Dylan gave her a quick lick on her hand. *Thanks!*

"I'll take it from here." She went to Harry. "Ready to roll?"

"Wait," Sumo blurted. "Harry took Canela from the stable. He used the road through the woods to get her to the horse trailer. We followed them here." He held up his cell phone. "You got to see this. I got Harry in the truck cab, Harry and Brandon fighting, Harry's confession, the whole thing on video."

"Thanks guys!" She gave them a mega grin. "This just became my favorite case."

Brandon added. "They did a great job."

"Incredible is more like it," Leslie said. "How were you able to do all that?"

"We're Dylan's Dog Squad. We do search and rescue," Sumo explained. "Dylan's got a great nose. He can find anyone or anything. That's how he found Canela and Harry." Sumo patted his cell phone. "I do social media."

"Here." Casey held out Harry's bandana. "Dylan found Harry's bandana on the trail. It proves he stole Canela."

"All this will be very useful at trial." Leslie took latex gloves out of one jacket pocket and an evidence bag out of the other. She slipped on the gloves, took the bandana from Casey, and dropped it into the evidence bag. She grinned at Harry. "I love this case."

"This is stupid," Harry snarled and stepped up to her. "You're stupid. I want a lawyer."

"Good idea," Leslie agreed. "You're going to need one. You've racked up a lot of charges. Conspiracy, horse stealing, assault, arson." Leslie's voice went hard as granite. "Now back up before I add threatening an FBI special agent."

"There's more," Casey broke in. "Harry hurt Dylan." Casey pointed to Sumo's cell phone. "You'll see it on the video."

Leslie rounded on Harry. "You *hurt* this cute, fluffy American Cocker Spaniel?"

You know I'm an American Cocker Spaniel! Dylan's heart leaped. *Finally, somebody knows!*

Leslie gave Harry a dead-eyed stare. "Now *that's* just wrong."

I agree. Whine.

Leslie slipped on her aviator sunglasses and cinched his handcuffs tighter.

"Ow!" Harry protested. "This is abuse. I'm going to file charges."

Dylan pawed the air at Leslie. *I like you.*

"You do that." Leslie handed her card to Sumo. "Stay

here. I'll send Special Agent Nevins over to get your cell phone."

"My cell phone!" Sumo yelped and hugged it to his chest.

"We'll make a copy of the video and get your cell phone back to you." She put one hand on Harry's shoulder and the other on top of the cuffs. "Harry Biggs, you have the right to remain silent," she began and walked him away.

"I guess that's it," Casey said.

"For now," Fernando agreed. "Harry will get a lawyer. We'll go to trial." He blew out a breath. "But I feel good about this one."

"It's so weird that you're the good guy," Sumo said. "You've been such a jerk."

"Part of my job." Brandon shoved both hands into his jeans pockets.

You helped save Nell. Dylan gave him a canine grin. *You're a good guy.*

"When Dad finds out about Harry, it's going to blow him away," Sumo said in a low voice. "Dad trusted him."

"The wild thing is Nell never trusted him." Casey hugged Dylan. "That's why she was always trying to get away from him."

No wonder she was always so nervous.

"I guess no one ever really knows anyone." Brandon thought a moment. "How'd you know the bandana belonged to Harry?"

"We didn't," Casey admitted. "Dylan found it in the woods and gave it to us. We forgot about it when you started fighting with Harry."

"Dylan knew Harry's smell and his smell was on the bandana," Sumo reasoned. "That's why he went after him."

Yup. Whine.

"Ho!" a man's voice called out.

Casey, Dylan, Sumo, and Brandon turned to watch a special agent walking Canela down the ramp. He kept one hand on her mane. "Steady, girl."

Brandon nodded in their direction. "They'll check Canela out and then she can go home."

I'm glad Nell gets to go home to Angelina. Dylan leaned against Casey's chest. *But I'm sad because I'll never see my friend again. Whine.*

Casey shifted Dylan in his arms. "Can Dylan say goodbye to Canela?"

"Sure. Because of Dylan a little girl is getting her horse back and we will make our case. He's a hero."

I like helping.

Brandon lightly tapped Dylan on his snout. "Harry had everyone fooled. It's amazing how Dylan knew it was him."

"It was easy." Casey smiled and hugged Dylan close. "Dylan's nose knows. Right, Little Buddy?"

Arf!

The End.

DYLAN RETURNS IN DYLAN'S MILLIONS
CHAPTER 1

"The State of California calls its first witness, Dylan Easter Donovan." Deputy District Attorney Silva nodded to Casey and Dylan seated in the courtroom audience." Please take the witness stand." She motioned them forward.

"That's us, Little Buddy." Casey scooped Dylan up.

Whine.

Mom patted Dylan's paw. "Don't worry. You'll be great."

"Go get the scumbag," Sumo said loudly. He raised his cell phone, video rolling. "Wait until Dylan's Dog Squad fans see this. I bet it goes viral."

The bailiff got to his feet and zeroed in on Sumo. Sumo got the hint and put his cell phone away.

Gasps sucked the air out of the courtroom and all heads turned to watch Casey and Dylan walk to the stand. Suddenly everyone was pointing and talking at once. It was deafening.

"Order in the courtroom!" Judge Beau banged his gavel.

Questions, fast and furious, exploded from the small group of reporters huddled in the first row.

"Seriously, Judge?" A woman reporter in a denim jacket shouted out. "The State's star witness is a dog?"

Dylan hooked his muzzle over Casey's shoulder and gave her a forty-two teeth canine grin. *That's me!*

A young guy with a ponytail and diamond chip earring cracked up. "My editor will love this. It'll be the lead story on the six o'clock news!"

Another reporter shook his head and typed like crazy on his iPad. "Only in California!"

The jury broke out in laughter. One woman, red-faced and giggling, reached into her purse for a tissue and wiped her eyes. A man covered his mouth, but his laugh escaped.

"Order! Order!" Judge Beau's gavel hammered out a rapid staccato on his bench.

Let's stay with Mom. Dylan nuzzled Casey's cheek. *Judge Beau looks mad.*

"It's okay, Little Buddy." Casey hugged Dylan close.

Judge Beau hunched forward in his black robe and put both elbows on his bench. His dark eyes flashed behind black horn-rimmed glasses. "One more outburst and I'll clear the courtroom." He shot his bailiff a look.

The bailiff stepped closer to the row of reporters, scowled, and gripped his gun belt with both hands.

"It's obvious my client can't get a fair trial in this court." Public Defender Zamsky glared at Ms. Silva. "Letting this dog testify is just plain stupid."

Judge Beau slowly took off his glasses, folded them and tapped them on the yellow legal pad in front of him. His voice dropped an octave. "Counselor, are you attacking the wisdom of this court?"

"Uh." Mr. Zamsky's face went milk white, and he put both hands on the counsel table to steady himself. "No, Judge!" His Adam's apple bobbed up and down. "I, I."

Judge Beau gave him a thin-lipped smile. "I will allow Dylan's testimony." He nodded to the court reporter. "Swear in the witness."

An ancient, tiny woman with a pinched face, a tight bun and orthopedic shoes stepped in front of Casey and Dylan. "Raise your right hand and state your name for the record."

Dylan right pawed the air and then glanced up at Casey. *A little help here.*

The news reporters elbowed each other out of the way to get pictures. A Pulitzer prize was in their future.

"This is Dylan Easter Donovan," Casey offered.

The tiny woman wasn't finished. "Do you swear to tell the truth, the whole truth and nothing but the truth?"

Arf!

The reporters fell over each other getting the sound bite for the six o'clock news.

"You may be seated," Judge Beau instructed.

Casey slid into the witness chair and settled Dylan on his lap.

"Ms. Silva," Judge Beau nodded, "please begin."

"Casey, are you Dylan's owner?"

"We own each other."

Arf! We're a team.

Muffled giggles and sighs swept through the courtroom.

Mr. Zamsky was again on his feet. "Casey needs to be sworn in too."

Without waiting to be summoned the tiny court reporter appeared next to Casey. "Raise your right hand and state your name for the record."

"Casey Donovan."

"Do you swear to tell the truth, the whole truth and nothing but the truth?"

Casey spoke into the microphone, "Yes."

"Your Honor," Mr. Zamsky protested. "This, this witness is a *dog!*"

Dylan sat up straighter on Casey's lap. *I'm an American Cocker Spaniel.*

"The court is aware." Judge Beau peered over the top of his black, horn-rimmed glasses. "What is your point, Mr. Zamsky?"

"Ms. Silva is using tricks to win her case. My client is innocent."

"No tricks, Judge Beau," Ms. Silva broke in. "Our case is simple. Go ahead Casey."

"Dylan and I were walking by Robina's Jewelers at the Brea Mall. We saw a guy wearing a ski mask and gloves. He smashed a glass jewelry case with a hammer and the store alarm went off."

It was really loud. Whine.

Casey stroked Dylan's ears. "The guy dropped the hammer and made a break for it. We ran after him and saw him toss his ski mask and gloves into a trash can. I got them out of the trash." Casey faced the judge. "My Uncle Rory is a Detective Lieutenant with Brea PD, so I knew they were important." He turned back to Ms. Silva. "Anyway, I showed the ski mask to Dylan and gave him the scent. We chased the guy to the Brea Mall Food Court. I called 9-1-1 and Dylan kept him cornered until Brea Police came."

"Dylan is a brave dog," a lady juror in a yellow blouse said to the man next to her.

"Really brave," the man agreed.

"My client, Otis Phipps, was in line at the *very crowded* Brea Mall Food Court. *This dog*," Mr. Zamsky pointed at Dylan, "just started barking at the first guy he came to. It doesn't prove my client tried to rob the jewelry store."

I did not. Mr. Phipps did too. Whine.

"Your Honor, Dylan is a trained search and rescue dog. This is Exhibit A." Ms. Silva offered a manila folder. "You will learn Dylan is American Kennel Club Canine Good Citizen certified and knows American Sign Language. Dylan, Casey Donovan, their best friend, Sumo Modragon —also known as Dylan's Dog Squad, have found missing kids, a stolen horse, and many criminals."

Judge Beau took the folder and read the report inside. "Continue, Ms. Silva."

"Big deal. So, the dog's been lucky." Mr. Zamsky sat down in his chair and sent Ms. Silva a pitying look. "There's no way Ms. Silva can prove Otis Phipps did this."

"Actually," Ms. Silva gave Mr. Zamsky a mega smile, "Dylan can."

"Very well," Judge Beau said. "Proceed."

"Your Honor!" Mr. Zamsky was back on his feet.

Judge Beau tossed his glasses onto the legal pad and rubbed the bridge of his nose. "You wanted proof, you're getting it."

"Gentlemen," Ms. Silva nodded to the bailiff and the court clerk.

The men opened the hallway door behind the judge's bench and rolled in a long screen. They angled the screen, blocking the view to the hallway. Everyone in the courtroom sat up and craned their necks. Four pairs of identical shoes shuffled in behind the screen.

Ms. Silva showed Casey a clear bag. "Do you recognize this?"

"It's the ski mask the guy dropped in the trash can when he ran out of Robina's Jewelers."

"Earlier you said you gave Dylan the scent." She handed him the bag. "Can you show us?"

"Sure." Casey turned Dylan to him, put out both arms and tapped his right fist on his left wrist, signing Work. "Dylan let's go to work."

Dylan sprang off Casey's lap. He waited for Casey and then they walked in front of the judge's bench. Dylan sat, keeping his eyes on Casey.

"Dylan has an amazing nose. He can find anyone or anything." Casey crouched beside Dylan and showed him the ski mask. "Dylan, this is Otis. Dylan find Otis."

The courtroom went quiet. Men and women leaned forward in their seats. All eyes were on Dylan.

Dylan snuffled the ski mask and whined.

"Ha! What did I tell you." Mr. Zamsky smirked to the jurors. "This is just some dumb trick."

"Dylan, this is Otis. Dylan find Otis," Casey repeated.

Dylan raised his snout and scented the air. Then he padded toward the screen.

"Oh." The crowd murmured.

"Quiet in the courtroom," the bailiff ordered.

"Can he really smell the guy?" An elderly juror blurted out and put on his glasses. "I got to see this."

Dylan stopped at the first pair of shoes. *Nope.* His nose quivered and his lips curled. *But you stepped in something really yucky.* He moved to the next and hesitated. *Not you.* He kept his nose low and went to the third pair. *Smells like grass.*

"He can't do it," Robina from Robina's Jewelers groaned from the third row. "Now that creep will go free."

I'm not done yet. Dylan flicked an ear and went to the next pair of shoes. *Hmm.* Dylan sniffed over the shoes and his nose traveled up the man's pant leg. He inhaled deeply.

The man shook his leg out. Dylan went to the man's other pant leg and sniffed. *Now I am.* He sat and alerted. *Arf!*

Casey went to Dylan, knelt and twisted both hands in the air, signing Yay. "Good job, Little Buddy!"

Arf!

The bailiff and court clerk removed the screen. Three men looked to the judge. The fourth man glared at Mr. Zamsky. "Hey! Are you gonna just sit there or what?"

"So much for man's best friend," a female reporter laughed out loud.

"Let the record show," Ms. Silva stated, "Dylan identified Otis Phipps."

The courtroom cheered and Judge Beau pounded his gavel. The spectators ignored him and cheered louder. Judge Beau frowned. He raised his gavel again but gave up and let the people have their way.

"I object!" Mr. Zamsky shouted to be heard. "This little trick didn't prove anything."

Now Ms. Silva sent him a pitying look. "Because of Dylan's amazing nose Mr. Phipps was arrested at the Brea Mall and now he'll be convicted." She smiled at Dylan. "Everyone knows a dog's nose is superior to humans."

Thank you. Dylan snuffled his Dylan's Dog Squad bandana. *Just doing my job.*

She tipped her head toward Mr. Zamsky. "Your client just happens to be a lousy criminal and got caught."

Yup.

Ms. Silva turned to the jury. "I rest my case."

Judge Beau banged his gavel once. "We'll take a fifteen-minute recess." He paused. "Casey, Dylan, Sumo, and Ms. Donovan, please join me in chambers." He left the bench without looking back.

Dylan pawed at Casey's leg. *Are we in trouble?*

"Ms. Donovan. Sumo." The bailiff waited for Casey and Dylan to join them. "This way."

"What is this about," Mom asked.

The bailiff shrugged. "Judge Beau didn't tell me."

They followed the bailiff down a narrow hallway past closed doors. At a partially opened mahogany door, the bailiff stopped, knocked once, and stood back to let them enter.

Judge Beau was already seated at his desk. His long black robe was hung on a coatrack and the sleeves of his white shirt were rolled up. "Please sit down."

Sumo claimed the first chair. Casey sat in the one next to him and put Dylan on his lap. Mom took the last chair.

Mom asked, "Is something wrong?"

"Not at all." Judge Beau smiled.

You look nicer when you smile. Dylan gave him a canine grin. *Most people do.*

"It's a small world, Ms. Donovan. I'm told you have a children's book business, and you represent authors and illustrators."

Mom's eyebrows arched. "Yes."

Judge Beau swiveled in his chair and tapped a key on his computer. A craggy faced, whitehaired man with watery blue eyes filled the screen.

"Cranky Pants!" Casey and Sumo said together.

What's he doing here?

"Cranston Pantswick," Mom corrected and gave them The Look. She turned back to the screen. "Cranston this is a surprise."

"Horace and I go way back. Before I became the biggest, most powerful children's book publisher in North America, I was only a man with a dream. Horace was a young lawyer and he helped me start my business. We stayed friends." Cranston brought his wrinkled face closer to the screen. "Where's Dylan?" He turned his face this way and that for a look. "Does Dylan want to say hello to his Uncle Cranston?"

No. Dylan pressed himself against Casey's chest. *Don't let him see me.*

"It's always nice to see you, Cranston," Mom tried for pleasant, "but you could've called."

Cranky Pants brushed that aside. "Colleen, do you want to go to Yosemite National Park?"

"No."

Cranky Pants frowned. "That's ridiculous. Of course, you do."

"Yosemite!" Casey and Sumo fist bumped and grinned.

"Here it comes," Sumo whispered. "Wait for it. Wait for it."

Wait for what?

"Cranky Pants always gets his way," Casey whispered to Dylan.

"No Cranston I definitely do not." Now Mom frowned. "Yosemite has mosquitos, hiking, camping, hot summer temperatures and *nature*."

I like those things. Dylan looked at the strappy gold sandals on Mom's feet. *You don't.*

Cranky Pants spoke over her. "Yosemite is the perfect place for my new book. I want to inspire boys and girls to spend time in the fresh air." He thumped a bony fist on the table in front of him. Water jumped in his glass. "Children today know nothing, nothing I tell you of the great outdoors. They spend all their time on their phones." He gave a long sniff with enough suction to make a vacuum proud.

"Like you've ever spent any time in the outdoors," Mom said under her breath.

"What?" his blue eyes snapped to hers.

"I said," Mom cleared her throat, "you love spending time outdoors."

"Because of my book children will learn the basics of camping. Study the forest. Discover wildlife." Cranky Pants was on a roll and his gnarly hand traced an arc the air. "I'm calling my new book, *The Wonders of Yosemite*." He winked. "I need the best illustrators. Hire Priscilla Burris and Gina Capaldi."

"I'm truly sorry," Mom jumped in. "They're working on another book."

"What?" Happiness was gone. "You're telling me you're too busy for my little book?"

"Of course not," Mom soothed. "Your book is a wonderful idea. It sounds lovely."

Cranston finger tapped the computer screen. "If you organized your time better, this wouldn't be a problem."

Mom sighed. "I've never let you down."

Casey and Sumo huddled together and high-fived.

"Yosemite here we come!" Sumo whispered.

Casey hugged Dylan again and whispered, "This will be a blast, Little Buddy."

Arf!

Joy flashed across Cranky Pants' lined face. "Dylan! You're here!"

I should've kept my arf to myself. Dylan hunkered down on Casey's lap. *Save me.*

Judge Beau faced them. "This sounds like an excellent opportunity for your business, Ms. Donovan."

"Fine, Cranston." Mom opened the calendar app on her phone. "When shall we meet to discuss this?"

"We just did. Pay attention, Colleen!" Cranky Pants

white bushy eyebrows dipped into one long row. "You leave on Thursday."

"Tomorrow? No." Mom shook her head. "I can't possibly."

"No excuses." Cranky Pants ticked-tocked his index finger back and forth. "You work from home. I've made all the arrangements. Your itinerary is being emailed to you as we speak. My daughter Sasha will be your photographer."

"Sumo's mother is in Italy. I don't have her permission."

"No problem," Cranky Pants scoffed. "He's always with you and Casey."

True. Dylan nosed Casey's hand. *Sumo wishes he had a mom like ours.*

Sumo waved his hand in the air to get his attention. "How are we going to get there?"

"Clever lad! You remind me of myself at your age." Cranky Pants' eyes crinkled at the corners. "Smart people are always concerned with details. My limousine will pick you up at seven tomorrow morning and take you to John Wayne Airport."

I love riding in Cranky Pants' limo. Dylan faced Casey. *He always has junk food.* Dylan's pink tongue licked his lips. *I love junk food.*

"Do we get to fly in your private jet," Casey asked.

"Casey!" Mom rolled her eyes.

"It's so cool Mom!"

Dylan pawed the air. *It is!*

Cranky Pants sighed. "Mariposa-Yosemite Airport is a private airport and too small for my Gulfstream 550 to fly into. Luckily Sasha is a licensed pilot. She's chartered a small plane." He grinned. "The flight is about two hours. You'll be able to discuss the photo shoots with her during the trip."

"Great," Mom said through clenched teeth.

Judge Beau broke in. "You forgot to tell Ms. Donovan my brother Edmund is famous. He knows everything there is to know about Yosemite National Park. He also has a whitewater rafting business on the Tuolumne River."

Two wah la me. That's a funny name.

"Oh wow!" Casey and Sumo said.

"His granddaughter lives with him," Judge Beau added. "She's about your age and can show you what there is to do."

"That sounds like fun," Casey said.

Judge Beau gave a half laugh. "You haven't met her yet."

Yikes.

PARTS OF THE HORSE AND HORSE EQUIPMENT

- BARREL: The area behind the girth area to the flank. Beneath is the ribcage that surrounds the horse's vital organs.
- CINCH: A strap that holds a saddle on a horse.
- CURRY BRUSH: A rubbery brush useful in removing dirt, old hair, and debris from the horse. It can be used nearly all over and should be used in a circular motion. Do not use on the horse's face or inside its legs.
- DANDY BRUSH: A brush with long, stiff bristles used to remove the dirt and other debris brought up by the curry brush.
- FILLY: A young female horse usually less than four years old.
- FLANK: The slightly indented area behind the area of the barrel. This is the area to watch to count the horse's respiration.
- FORELOCK: The part of the horse's mane that falls forward between the ears and onto the forehead.

- HALTER: Headgear that fits behind the ears, and around the muzzle. To handle the horse a lead rope is usually attached.
- HANDS: Also known as HANDS HIGH: A hand is a measuring unit. A hand represents four inches or approximately the width of a male adult's hand.
- HEEL: The back side of the hoof.
- HOOF: The horny part of the horse's foot.
- LEAD ROPE: A rope attached to a halter with a heavy clip or snap to lead a horse.
- LUNGE LINE: The handler moves the horse around in a circle at a walk, trot, or canter. This is typically done to burn off excess energy before riding the horse or to do an exercise between riding sessions.
- MANE: The hair that grows from the top of the neck of a horse to the withers and includes the forelock.
- MUZZLE: The part of the horse's head that includes the area of the mouth, nostrils, chin, lips, and front of the nose.
- PALOMINO: A pale golden or tan-colored horse or pony with a white mane and tail, originally bred in the southwestern United States.
- PONY: Anything less than 14.2 hands tall is considered a pony.
- ROUND PEN: A round, enclosed pen allowing more interaction between horse and handler and more control over the horse because the horse can't fully avoid its handler.

- QUARTER HORSE: A horse of a small, stocky breed noted for agility and speed over short distances. It is considered to be the fastest breed of horse over distances of a quarter of a mile.
- SORREL: A reddish coat color in a horse lacking any black. It is synonymous with chestnut and one of the most common colors in horses.
- WITHERS: The highest part of a horse's back, lying at the base of the neck above the shoulders. The height of a horse is measured to the withers.
- YEARLING: A young male or female horse between one and two years old.

RECIPES

TRADITIONAL S'MORES

Ingredients

- 8 large marshmallows
- 1 4.4 ounce milk chocolate bar, broken into 8 pieces
- 8 whole graham crackers, broken into squares

Directions

1. Put a marshmallow on a skewer and set a stovetop burner or outdoor grill to low heat. Very carefully turn the marshmallow over the heat for 1 to 2 minutes until the marshmallow slightly puffs and begins to turn brown, or to your desired doneness. Repeat with remaining marshmallows.

2. Place each piece of chocolate onto one graham cracker square. When the marshmallows are toasted, carefully remove from the skewers and place on top of the chocolate. Place the second graham cracker square on top of the marshmallow and squish down to melt the marshmallow into the chocolate.
3. Enjoy!

PEANUT BUTTER COOKIE S'MORES

Follow the above recipe and directions but substitute peanut butter cookies for the graham crackers.

SIMPLE SIGNS/HAND COMMANDS

APPLAUSE/YAY: Hold your hands in the air and twist them a couple of times.

COME: Extend both hands with index fingers pointing forward and up.
　　Then bend your arms at the elbow, pull your fingers in toward your body.

DAD: Open your fingers and place your thumb on your temple.

(DIRECTIONS) LEFT: Raise hand and show thumb and index finger only. Motion to the left.

(DIRECTIONS) RIGHT: Raise hand, show index and third fingers only. Cross index and third fingers. Motion to the right.

DOWN: Point your index finger down and move your hand in a downward direction.

GO: This is done by 'throwing' the index fingers forward. The index fingers trace the air. Throwing the index fingers to the side is popular, too.

HI: Open hand to forehead and quickly move away in a salute.

HIPPO: Extend your index finger and little finger on both hands, and open and close them, having both hands meet in the middle—like a hippo's mouth.

I DON'T KNOW: Shrug your shoulders.

I LOVE YOU: Show your little finger, then your index finger and then your thumb.

LISTEN: Raise right hand, curl down third, fourth and fifth fingers. Point index finger straight up and point thumb to ear.

JUMP: Make one hand flat. With your other hand, extend your middle and index fingers to make a 'little man' and have him jump up and down on your flat hand.

MOM: Open your fingers and place your thumb on your chin.

NO: Take your first two fingers and tap them with your thumb, resembling a mouth talking.

NOT ME: Point index finger to chest and shake your head no.

SIMPLE SIGNS/HAND COMMANDS

(ARE YOU) OKAY: Point the index finger on your dominant hand toward the person and then quickly withdraw your index finger. With your thumb straight up, make a couple of quick circles.

PLEASE: Put your dominant hand on your chest with your thumb sticking out and your fingers extended. Move your hand in a circular motion (clockwise) two or three times.

PROMISE: Closed hand with index finger extended and touching mouth. Move hand forward and down while opening to rest on open up-turned palm of other hand.

QUIET: Bring your index finger to your lips.

SERIOUSLY: Make a serious face. Place tip of dominant index finger on chin and twist clockwise.

SHOW ME: Open left hand with fingers separated. Then point to the center of your palm with right index finger.

SIT DOWN: Have one hand flat/palm up. Take your other hand with index and middle fingers extended together in a slight hook to make the person's legs, and then sit them on your open palm.

STAY: Use your thumb and little finger in a palm-down 'Y' shape. The movement is a forward thrust, not a downward slap. You are shoving the knuckles forward and a bit down.

STOP: Extend your left hand, palm upward. Bring your right hand down to your left hand at a right angle.

THANK YOU: Take the inside of your dominant hand, touching your fingertips to your lips and then move it slightly down and toward the person you are talking to.

WATCH: Use your index and third fingers. Thrust them forward.

WORK: Close both hands into fists in front of you, then tap your right fist on top of your left fist a couple of times in the wrist area.

YES: Take a hand and make it into a fist and bob it back and forth.

ACKNOWLEDGMENTS

A dog's sense of smell is 10,000 to 100,000 times better than a human's. The reason is pretty simple: For every scent receptor a human has, a dog has about 50. A fun fact is dogs with shorter noses typically do better than other dogs at following a scent. When Dylan was going through training, his instructors wanted to know how he could keep up with Labradors, Bloodhounds, Beagles, and the other super dogs in his class. (Dylan was always the only American Cocker Spaniel.) My answer was always the same: Dylan's nose knows. He could follow any scent, but his favorite was to Baskin-Robbins vanilla ice cream—his reward at the end of a working day.

Many thanks to Gina Capaldi, award winning illustrator, author, and dear friend, for not once complaining about the zillion photographs, I sent to her of Dylan. Her cover designs for *Dylan's Dilemma, Dylan's Dream, Dylan's Villain, Dylan's Hawaiian Ghost* and *Dylan's Nose Knows* are perfect and I can't thank her enough. They make my heart sigh.

Many thanks to Billy da Pug and his wonderful mum, Leslie Linares. Billy da Pug was the winner of our very first Dylan's Dog Squad contest. Originally, the winner was to only have a mention in *Dylan's Nose Knows*, but then I met Billy da Pug. I immediately fell in love and knew he had to have a bigger part. He's every bit as adorable as his character in the story.

Many thanks to my best friend Robyn Matias for her constant support and never telling me once that I should stick to my day job.

Many thanks to my incredibly talented writers and illustrators' group: Teri Vitters, Priscilla Burris, and Gina Capaldi. Their work leaves me speechless.

Many thanks to Jonathan and Jynafer Yanez, Archimedes Books, for guiding me through the boggling process of getting my book published. You are truly amazing, and I am grateful for you every day.

Many thanks to Retired Detective Lieutenant Kelly Carpenter, Brea Police Department, for patiently answering my endless questions about police procedure.

Many thanks to Deborah Halverson and her invaluable editing comments.

Many thanks to Heidi Campbell, horse trainer and lesson instructor. For eight long weeks she endured my nonstop questions about horses, horse care and horse training. If there is something she doesn't know about horses, it isn't worth knowing.

Many thanks to Joe and Teri Beattie for sharing their horses and love of horses with me. If I were a horse, I would want to live with them.

Many thanks to Rita Carda Native American consultant, for her knowledge of Native Americans, their customs and their contributions.

Many thanks to Captain Chris Marvin, Brea Fire Department, for always being willing to answer my questions and offer advice about fire procedures and the joys of owning a boat.

I couldn't have done this without you.

ABOUT DYLAN EASTER TROY

Dylan was born on Easter in Daejeon, South Korea. His owner bought him from Walmart. At that time, I suggested basic dog training, but his owner didn't think training was important. Dylan immediately destroyed his owner's apartment by chewing his way through electrical coverings, baseboards, and furniture. When Dylan ate the interior of his owner's BMW, his owner decided having a dog was too much work and didn't want him anymore.

I said I would take him.

Dylan spent twenty-seven hours in a plane's cargo hold to get to California. When I picked him up at Korean Air Cargo, Los Angeles International Airport, he was eighteen months old, didn't know his own name, and was not housebroken. We immediately started training and Dylan thrived. He loved agility training and competing with other dogs. His first big step came when he became certified as a Therapy Dog. Dylan enjoyed that job but when he became American Kennel Club Canine Good Citizen certified, he went into service dog training and became a Hospice Service Dog for people actively dying.

Additionally, Dylan's accomplishments include:

- Bilingual understanding: English and Korean
- Five hundred word and phrase vocabulary
- Basic American Sign Language and hand commands
- Ability to contact 9-1-1 with a special device
- Count to ten
- Television appearances
- Recognized in a feature article in *The Orange County Register* for his accomplishments
- Recognized by Baskin-Robbins for his accomplishments and his love of their vanilla ice cream
- Mascot for Cypress College in Cypress, California.

Dylan is proof that there are no bad dogs. In fact, he's the smartest, best dog I've ever had or ever trained. Dogs need love, guidance, companionship, and a sense of purpose. At the end of Dylan's workday, he received a bit of Baskin-Robbins vanilla ice cream.

He deserved it.

ABOUT THE AUTHOR

KATHLEEN TROY, JD; PHD

Kathleen Troy is a published author, children's book publisher, movie producer, writing and law professor at Cypress College, and former Director of Education and Development for the Archdiocese of Los Angeles. Kathleen is an active member of Sisters in Crime and Society of Children's Book Writers and Illustrators and has won several awards for middle grade and young adult books. Dog training is Kathleen's passion, and she has achieved recognition, most notably for training service dogs for hospice work.

Kathleen welcomes hearing from you. Please get in touch with her at www.kathleentroy.com.

STAY INFORMED

I'd love to stay in touch! You can email me at kathleen@kathleentroy.com

For updates about new releases, as well as exclusive promotions, visit my website and sign up for the VIP mailing list. Head there now to receive a free story

www.kathleentroy.com

Enjoying the series? Help others discover *Dylan's Dog Squad* by sharing with a friend.

Printed in the USA
CPSIA information can be obtained
at www.ICGtesting.com
JSHW022031060324
58449JS00004B/22